A Rhyming History of Britain

55BC–AD1966

A Rhyming
History of
Britain

55BC–AD1966

JAMES MUIRDEN

ILLUSTRATIONS BY

DAVID ECCLES

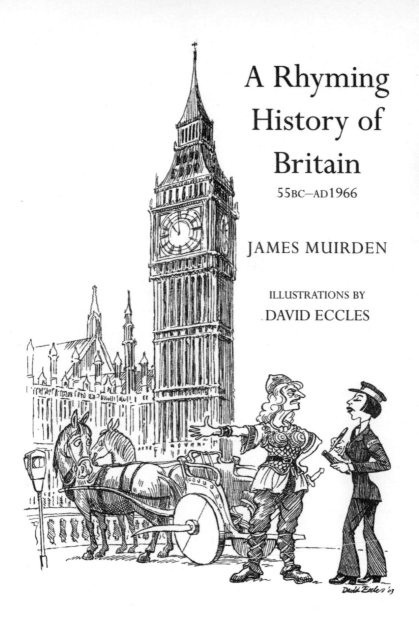

Robinson

London

Constable & Robinson Ltd
3 The Lanchesters
162 Fulham Palace Road
London W6 9ER
www.constablerobinson.com

First published in the UK by Constable,
an imprint of Constable & Robinson Ltd 2003

This paperback edition published by Robinson,
an imprint of Constable & Robinson Ltd 2006

A copy of the British Library Cataloguing in
Publication data is available from the British Library

ISBN-13: 978-1-84529-277-5 (pbk)
ISBN-10: 1-84529-277-4

ISBN-10: 1-84119-632-0 (hbk)

Printed and bound in the EU

1 3 5 7 9 10 8 6 4 2

James Muirden has written some thirty books on astronomy and space, and in addition has been a film reviewer and telescope maker. He is currently studying the astronomical orientation of medieval churches. Married with two children, he lives in Devon.

> Four lines I'm granted to describe my life –
> No need for more, as far as I can see!
> I've got two children and a wife
> And don't take any sugar in my tea.

Contents

For Dan and Emma

whose lives will occupy
several subsequent stanzas

Introduction

I am not a historian. In fact, I wrote this poem in order to teach myself some history. I thought that sorting facts into verse form would concentrate my mind wonderfully. Which it did!

I end my history in 1966 – the year of swinging London, when England won the World Cup. It was also the year when a phase of my own life ended, and I left that lofty Victorian house in Earls Court, London, where I had lived since the end of the war, when I was three.

My parents ran it as a boarding house. It was a remarkable boarding house, because people came only on recommendation, and usually stayed for years – until they finished their course of study, or got married, or changed jobs. Everyone ate together at an immense table in the basement dining room, and my mother cooked vast meals at which there were always 'seconds'. She sat at the end nearest the kitchen, and my father sat at the end nearest the window, and on Sunday lunchtimes he carved a ponderous, fat-drizzled joint of beef that had been brought to the subterranean tradesmen's entrance by the butcher's boy on his bicycle.

Some of the names who sat at that table achieved transient fame (such as the film actress Nancy Kwan); enduring fame (Richard Adams and Michael Holroyd – Michael never lived with us, but was friendly with a lodger, and would 'come to tea') or fatal fame (the only one, as far as I know– David Blakely, subsequently murdered by Ruth Ellis, the last woman to be hanged). And there was the champion of Lutyens and Victorian Gothic, the architect Roderick Gradidge, then a student, who at some point in the Fifties persuaded my accommodating father to paint his ceiling dark green. It came as a shock, not long ago, to open the *Guardian* and find myself looking at his obituary.

I have always associated Roderick with the *Cautionary Verses* of Hilaire Belloc, perhaps because I can still hear and see him bursting with mirth as he quoted from them; and delighting in those poems as a youngster drummed their simple and jolly iambic tetrameters into my head, where they have te-tum-tetummed away ever since:

> Matilda[1] told such Dreadful Lies
> It made one Gasp and Stretch one's Eyes ...

So when I started on what I hoped would be a simple and jolly history, the form preceded the content. At a personal level, these couplets gallop over the bridge between the ending of my life in that extended family and the moment when I decided to write this rhyming history of the times that preceded it.

---

[1] Or Maud (pp. 33–5)

Belloc's ironic verses usually ended with a Moral — in the case of George, whose balloon burst and caused the family house to collapse, it was that

> ... little Boys
> Should not be given dangerous Toys.

Had he been alive today he might have enjoyed, or at least appreciated, the double irony of predicting a society so constrained by regulation and litigation that even conkers are now considered Dangerous Toys. Will balloons be next?

I was encouraged to write this book by Carol O'Brien, of Constable & Robinson; and it would have taken much longer without the help of my wife Helen, who had the answers to most of my historical questions and, being a librarian, knew where to look for the others. The finished poem found the perfect illustrator in David Eccles, whose genius took root in my rough compost and flowered gloriously.

JAMES MUIRDEN

Celts and Saxons 55BC–AD927

To start this Rhyming History,
I've chosen 55 BC.
The Romans, who had got their hands
On all the European lands,
Could see this last annoying bit,
And thought they ought to conquer it.
Their famous Caesar, Julius,

Julius Caesar invaded
55 & 54 BC

Did not know what to make of us –
He couldn't work out who was who,
Since everyone was painted blue.
He took some souvenirs away,
Went home, and said 'Et tu, Brute?'

Caesar assassinated 44 BC

These folk were Celts, who, years before,
Had crossed the Channel to our shore –
Brave hostages of wind and tide,
And feeling rather sick inside.

c.700 BC

The Bronze Age Britons had to flee
Their cutting-edge technology,
For these Celts ushered in the stage
That's now known as the Iron Age.
Their priests, the Druids, seem to us
Malevolent and barbarous
(Though Stonehenge, coupled with their
      name,
Was defunct long before they came).

A century went by, and then
The Romans pestered us again.
Their new attack made better headway:
The crucial Battle of the Medway
(Not far from where the M2 crosses)
Was fought out with tremendous losses.

Emperor Claudius
invaded AD43

But once the Roman troops broke through,
There wasn't much the Celts could do,
Though people like Caratacus   40-52
And Boudicca made such a fuss   60-61
You'd think they didn't *want* to feel
Ground down beneath a foreign heel.

The Romans, in their Roman way,
Got down to work without delay.
Roads led to London, chief of ports,
While legions, garrisoned in forts,
Saw raiders off along the coast.
The northern tribes annoyed them most,
So Hadrian got lots of stone
And built his wall (well, not alone).   Hadrian's Wall c. 130
Selected fast-track Celts were sent
To seminars in management,
And also practised how to chat in
The civil service newspeak – Latin.

Thus, from a race which, let's admit,
Was practically illiterate
(They retold stories short and tall,
And kept no paperwork at all),
Came servants of the Roman state
To audit and administrate.
Their villas, in the latest styles,
Encrusted with mosaic and tiles,
Included features far excelling
Your plain bog-standard Celtic dwelling.
Piped water gurgled into bowls,
And sewage disappeared down holes.

But this secure life depended
On keeping Britain well defended;
And when the soldiers went back home
To fight the hordes that threatened Rome   401–2
Our frontiers were left quite bare,
And caved in almost everywhere.
From Ireland came Scots (I've checked,
So take it from me that's correct),
While out of Scotland Picts poured forth
And went rampaging through the north.
But Anglo-Saxons from the Rhine
Were where most people drew the line.

It was a dismal time indeed!
These Saxons were a fearful breed,
And if they came across a town,
Their policy was: 'Burn it down!'
The Celts did not know how to fight
These folk who set their homes alight,
For centuries of Roman law
Had left them ill-equipped for war.
So, with no viable defence,
A friendly posture made most sense –
Which means that most of us today
Contain some Celtic DNA.

c. 450–600
The Dark Ages appear to be
A time of total anarchy,
Almost unchronicled, we think,
Because the monks ran out of ink.
The little that we're sure of, lies
Beneath much guesswork and surmise.
King Arthur and his Celtic knights

Are one of fancy's finer flights:
Their exploitation has persisted,
Despite no proof that they existed –
Though evidence has now been found
That tables then *were* sometimes round.

During those years of doubt and dread,
The Christian faith began to spread
(Though it had started to impinge
Upon the so-called Celtic Fringe
During the Roman occupation).
It was a work of dedication:
c. 450   One Celtic Christian, Patrick, went
To Ireland, while some were sent
To wild lands beyond the Humber –
521-97   This team included St Columba.
But still most Anglo-Saxons swore
By heavy tacklers such as Thor.

8

When local zeal had lost all hope,
They got some backing from the Pope,   Pope Gregory r. 590–604
Who did his best to help their fight
And show these pagan souls the light.
Augustine led a delegation: 597
A man of utmost veneration –
Though maybe, later on, surprised
When posthumously canonized.
(Two saints share this illustrious name.
The other earned the greater fame
By praying, to relieve his worry:
'Lord, make me chaste – but there's no hurry'.)   Augustine of Hippo 354–430

Augustine managed to convert
The king of Kent, called Ethelbert,
Who met him in the open air
To keep an eye on who was there.
So Canterbury was the base
From which the movement grew apace –
A status it retains today.
The saintly mission worked away,
Inspired by a will divine
To bring more kingdoms into line.
They could, with justice, claim success:
The realm was Christian, more or less.

One faith; but on the other hand,
Too many kingdoms shared the land –
Divided rule could never be
A basis for security.
So now the Vikings rowed and baled
(And no doubt swam, if all else failed)

From c. 790   To reach our unprotected coast,
And see which one could rape the most –
The Danes, especially, had a craze
For active package holidays.
They toppled kingdoms one by one:
Another problem had begun.

By now, the Saxons must have felt
What it was like to be a Celt
When their own hordes began to pour
Across the land in days of yore.
Although they did their level best,
The Danes swept on towards the West,
Where Alfred, culinary king
Of Wessex, told his friends to bring
Whatever manpower they had got,
And they'd make mincemeat of the lot.
Too late, the Danes saw their mistake:
This wouldn't be a piece of cake.

Hungry for action, both sides met

878 At Edington, in Somerset.

King Guthrum, leader of the Danes,

Was quickly racked with stomach pains:

He skipped the pudding, praised the cook,

Known as the 'Peace of Wedmore'

And swore upon the Holy Book

To change his ways. Eventually

They sorted out a boundary

Along the Thames, then north to meet

The A5, known as Watling Street.

It went through Milton Keynes, past

Leicester,

Then took the right fork up to Chester.

This so-called Peace of London meant   ?881
A major new development:
For through its formal demarcation
It recognized the 'English' nation
As those who owned the south and west –
With Danelaw taking up the rest.
King Alfred wanted to be shot
Of this usurping Danish lot,
But realized it could not be done
Until the English fought as one.
The cornerstone, he clearly saw,
Would have to be a common law.

When Guthrum died, the treaty ended;   890
But England was now well defended
By mobile part-time troops, who went
Wherever there was harassment.   The 'fyrd'
Defence then turned into attack:
The Nordic hordes were driven back,
And Danelaw gradually receded
As Alfred's kingly heirs succeeded.
His grandson, Athelstan, completed
The reconquest, when he defeated
The northern Danes at York, to bring   Kingdom unified 927
The whole land under just one king.

Houses of Cerdic and Denmark 927—1066

ATHELSTAN 927–39

With Athelstan, England became
A realm in fact as well as name.
The Welsh chiefs and the Scottish kings
Were busy with their private things,
And Ireland was out of sight
(I'll say more when the time is right);
And though the Danes kept calling in
To see what trophies they could win,
No memorable name appears
In the succeeding forty years,

ETHELRED 978–1016

Till Ethelred, who, as you'll guess,
Was famous for Unreadiness.

He's earned a dismal reputation.
Corruption and procrastination
Blotted his reign; he even paid

'Danegeld'

The Danes vast sums not to invade.
His first wife died – she'd had enough –
But he knew of a bit of stuff,
Emma of Normandy, still single
Though sweet and twenty (and bilingual).
Her brother was the Duke, which meant
A pretty hefty settlement,

So she was fetched to share the bed
Of rough, unready Ethelred.

1002

Their married life was hardly bliss,
For everything had gone amiss.
The Dane Sweyn Forkbeard claimed the
    crown:
The royals rapidly left town,

Unsettled times 1013-16

Bought single tickets to Calais,
And had a welcome holiday.
When Ethelred came back again,
He and his son were duly slain,

EDMUND II Apr–Nov 1016

So now the Witan (council) got
Sweyn's son Canute to stop the rot

CANUTE 1016-35

(Who, incidentally, *never* tried
To order back the flowing tide).

This meant that Emma had to wait
On Brother's Normandy estate,
With Edward (son and king-to-be) –
Producing endless tapestry
And bored out of her tiny mind.
Canute now wrote to her, to find
If she could feel enough affection
To seal another French Connection.
No better offer was around:
She sailed back to be re-crowned,
With lots of needlework: meanwhile,
Young Edward stayed abroad, in exile.

Years passed, until his quiet life
Was shattered by the blare of strife.
Canute's enlightened reign had ended,
And now the country had descended
HAROLD I 1035–40   To bloody tumult, as his pair
Of sons disputed who was heir –
HARTHACNUT 1040–42   Within a few years both were dead,
Which knocked succession on the head.
The Witan noted down the name
Of anyone with any claim,
Since arrivistes with just a dribble
Of royal blood were eligible.

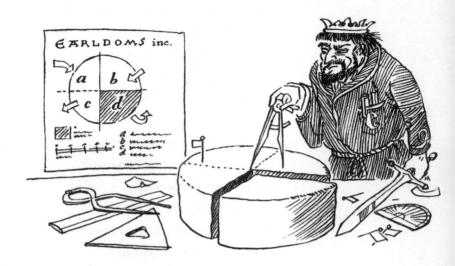

To help administer the law,
Canute had carved the place in four.
The earldoms he created were
East Anglia and Mercia;
Northumbria (to Humber's mouth);
And wealthy Wessex in the south.
Godwin, its scheming Earl, could see
That Edward, if he won, would be
A channel for his own ambition
To get his heirs the Top Position.
So he put Edward up for king
And canvassed votes like anything.

EDWARD (THE CONFESSOR)
1042–66

17

A king looks bare without a queen;
But Edward, who had always been
An earnest fellow, hardly sporty
(And very likely pushing forty),
Was not a prospect to excite
Much hope of sensual delight.
However, he was fitted out

Married in 1045   With someone he could take about:
Earl Godwin's daughter Edith, who
Some claimed he never really 'knew'.
The Godwins rubbed their hands with glee:
They'd got him in the family.

18

To thwart their power-seeking ends
He head-hunted some Norman friends
To work in his administration,
And paid the costs of relocation.
This caused the bitterest emotion
Among those side-stepped for promotion:
Why should he give those foreign yobs
Prestigious public-sector jobs?
The clash of cultures boiled over
One day (as it still does) at Dover,   1051
When Anglo-Saxons sorted out
Some Normans loitering about.

It almost came to civil war.
Whole armies were drawn up, before
The Godwins packed their bags and went
To winter on the Continent.
But what seemed absolute defeat
Was just a tactical retreat,
Since Edward, judging from report,
Was losing heavyweight support.
It gave them time to put together
A fleet, and wait for decent weather;
They came back with so many men,
He had to let them in again.

So now they had a major say
In what went on from day to day:
The Norman managers went back,
And one Archbishop got the sack.
With Edward's workload left so light,
He got hold of a building site
At Westminster, not far from town,

The first Westminster Abbey

And built a church (it's now knocked
     down):
A place where kings would be baptized,
And coronations solemnized.

Abbey consecrated 28 Dec 1065

The work was done, the paint had dried:

Edward died 4/5 Jan 1066

With nothing left to do, he died.

King Edward, known as the Confessor,
Was cagey over his successor,
And wouldn't give his name away
Until (it's said) his dying day.
William of Normandy was one   Later William the Conqueror
He'd probably have liked to run,
But after Dover, he could tell
No Norman had a hope in hell;
And who else would have had the clout
To keep the greedy Godwins out?
The new Earl, Harold, got his voice –   HAROLD II Jan–Oct 1066
It's known today as Hobson's Choice.

Duke William was distinctly miffed.
The crown ought to have been his gift:
The famous Bayeux Tapestry
Shows Harold swearing fealty.   Scenes 28 & 29 of the
Of course, it could have been designed   Tapestry
With such deceitful aims in mind,
Though facts that can and have been checked
Turn out remarkably correct.
Regardless of what Harold thought,
He knew a battle must be fought
Once he had been announced as king –
What would the Norman Conquest bring?

House of Normandy 1066—1154

Charlemagne r. 771–814

The Normans were a Nordic race
In urgent need of living-space,
Who grabbed, without a word of thanks,
Some land belonging to the Franks
(They'd swept right through the whole domain
Of Gaul, urged on by Charlemagne).
The Frankish kings, to their dismay,
Saw other districts break away,
Creating Flanders, Anjou, Maine,
And also wealthy Aquitaine.
From now on, these French realms will be
A part of Britain's history.

King Harold had big problems looming.
In Norman shipyards, trade was booming,
And up north there was nervous talk
Of Nordic plans to capture York:
Harold, the king of Norway (who
We'd better label Harold Two),
Had teamed up with the younger brother
Of Harold Number One (the other).
The heavens themselves would underline
These portents with a fearful sign:

Harold Hardraada

Tostig Godwinson

22

A comet, which shone out so bright
They screened a special *Sky At Night*.

Halley's Comet Apr 1066

Then came the news that Harold Two
Had taken York, so off One flew
(That's metaphorical, of course –
It took about a week by horse)
To play out this dramatic round
At Stamford Bridge, a neutral ground,
Collecting players on the way.
Against all odds, he won the day;

Battle of Stamford Bridge 25 Sep 1066

But they were hardly in the shower
When word arrived that William's power,
Landed near Hastings, must be crushed.

Pevensey Bay 28 Sep 1066

A pint or two, and off they rushed.

It may sound as if William made
That shrewd decision to invade
When Harold's army was up north –
The perfect time to venture forth.
In fact, he didn't have much say.
His ships would only go the way
The wind was blowing; if it faltered
They stopped; or (much worse) if it altered,
His expeditionary force,
Blown on to quite a different course,
Might now invade, thanks to the weather,
A different country altogether.

WILLELM III

As soon as Harold's lads got back
He launched a desperate attack,
At Battle, quite a way inland,
Where William's army made its stand.
The butchery went on all day.   14 Oct 1066
How Harold fell, we cannot say –
The 'arrow in the eye' could be
Unwarranted embroidery.   Bayeux Tapestry scenes 71-2
His mother, it was later told,
Offered his corpse's weight in gold.
'He isn't worth it,' William said:
'Get something for the house instead!'

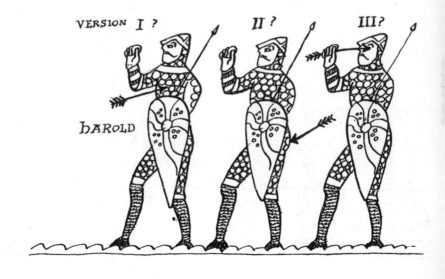

WILLIAM I 1066–87

King William wanted to create
An adjunct to the Norman State.
At Westminster, on Christmas Day,
He was crowned king; but on the way
He made clear his innate desire
To set each place he passed on fire.
Wherever his lieutenants went
Their dedicated efforts sent
Flames (and insurance costs) sky-high,
No doubt attracting passers-by,
To see what quadruped or chicken
Had been thus rendered finger-lickin'.

He knew he was the enemy
Of Saxon aristocracy:
The earls he banished in disgrace,
And Norman barons took their place.
Each one of these was told to build
A castle, which the owner filled
With knights (and paid their keep, of course),
Creating a repressing force
At the disposal of the king,
Which hadn't cost him anything.
But though rebellion could be scotched,
Armed barons needed to be watched.

The Tower and the Domesday Book
Were major tasks he undertook.
Beside the Thames he found a site,
With river views to left and right
And water buses on the hour,
On which he built his famous Tower.   Completed before 1100
Though called White, it's a dirty brown –
A high-rise block just out of town;
Though on his visits, he'd prefer
To stay with friends in Winchester.
The Tower would be used by kings
To house all sorts of awkward things.

27

1085–86

The Domesday Survey was so big
It counted every single pig
South of the Tees: this work was done
In twelve months flat. It was begun
Because he felt he really ought
To have meticulous report
Of what land everybody held,
Which set their dues in tax or 'geld'.
The two books (one was not enough)
Fall in the class of weighty stuff:
Page after page of Latin screed
That's quite impossible to read.

Kept in the
Public Record
Office

9 Sep 1087

King William, when he died, admitted
The dreadful crimes he had committed:
The countless English he'd subdued,
And slaughtered, starved, or barbecued.
But even so, his reign had brought
The order he so keenly sought,
And which would rapidly decay
When his two eldest had their way.

Robert got Normandy; the crown
Of England, though, was handed down
To William Rufus as his due –   WILLIAM II 1087–1100
So you can guess what that led to.

The brothers soon began to fight,
And went on, with no end in sight –
Blood-lettings, blindings, rapes, castrations,
And periodic conflagrations.
Portents appeared: a well ran red
Near the M4, at Finchampstead,
So when King William fell, shot through,
Did fate let loose the arrow too?   2 Aug 1100
In holy state (though he had lapsed)
They buried him. The church collapsed,   At Winchester
But not because of royal guilt:
The tower had been jerry-built.

Though William Rufus must have seen
A lot of flesh, he had no queen;
No legal issue of his own
Gave brother Robert England's throne.
Robert, however, was away
On an adventure holiday
That lasted for a year at least –
Crusading in the Middle East.
So when he got back home, he found

HENRY I 1100–35   His baby brother Henry crowned
(Who'd been adjacent to the spot
Where William Rufus had been shot).

Of all our documented kings,
Henry was wildest in his flings.
Lord knows how many maids he chased
(One in a bed seemed such a waste),
But it is proved he caught sufficient,
And then was suitably efficient
To make the population grow
By twenty – more, for all we know.
But once he'd got himself the crown,
And was advised to settle down,
He sired just two, as we shall see –
And both would bring him misery.

Enthroned, King Henry was aware
That brother Robert would go spare,
Raise up an army, launch a fleet,
And say they really ought to meet.
William had fleeced the church of land,
And taxed the barons out of hand,
But Henry very quickly saw
He'd need their help to fight this war,
And so he issued, as a starter,
His famous Coronation Charter.   5 Aug 1100
It promised everyone the moon –
Well, not quite yet, but pretty soon.

31

The king, however, had to face
Two rivals for his power base.
The barons first: the Conqueror's gift
Of lands was bound to cause a rift,
Since they were now in a position
Of local strength, and great ambition.
The church disliked the way the king
Could veto almost everything,
And choose the bishops he liked best –
A right which, later on, would test
To breaking-point (as we'll relate)

i.e. Henry II & Becket   The tensions between Church and State.

The brothers' war went Henry's way.
He captured Robert at Tinchebrai,   28 Sep 1106
Flung him into captivity,
And claimed the seat of Normandy.
This was a memorable date:
From then till 1558   The loss of Calais
The English crown would be obsessed
With the French duchies it possessed.
King Henry hardly ever came
To see the land he ruled in name:
Rough Saxon dogs, no *savoir faire* –
Why run the risk of *mal de mer*?

He did, however, look abroad
To find Matilda (known as Maud),
His Scottish queen, who soon gave birth
To what he wanted most on earth –
A son, the princely William, who
Wed Maud (Matilda?) of Anjou.
Will sailed from France upon the flood,
His White Ship filled with noble blood...
An unseen rock – need I say more?
A single sailor reached the shore.   25 Nov 1120
(Some of the crew were drunk: the manner
Of his sad death recalls Diana.)

We can conceive the king's despair.
He had no other male heir:
Though he and Maud (Matilda) tried,
All she could do before she died
Was bear Matilda (Maud), to be
His hope of continuity.
The husband Henry chose for her,
The Holy Roman Emperor,
Though head of an enormous nation,
Was not much good at procreation.
Matilda (Maud) tried Number Two:
Count Geoffrey, ruler of Anjou.

Now, since the Normans did not think
Rosé d'Anjou a pleasant drink,
Maud's husband was not to their taste.
Another challenge Henry faced
Was nephew Stephen, Count of Blois
(Tricky to rhyme, but there you are).
He'd wed the daughter of a lord,
Whose name just happened to be Maud,
Though also known as (try to guess).
So things were really in a mess:
Two sides convinced that they were right,
Engaging in a royal fight.

Though Stephen openly attested
Matilda ought to be invested,
Henry had not yet been interred
(His death, of course, can be inferred)
Before the bishops had him crowned   STEPHEN 1135–54
On Westminster's all-hallowed ground.
We can imagine Maud's dismay –
She, naturally, saw Rosé,
And plunged them into civil war,
Which brought the barons to the fore,
Since they alone had the resources
Of archers, armoured men and horses.

This English mayhem also meant
Confusion on the Continent,
And Normandy fell bit by bit
Till Maud and Geoff owned all of it.

Feb 1141   Matilda once laid hands on Stephen,
But he escaped, and got back even
By laying siege to her. Her flight
Dec 1142   (A secret rope at dead of night)
Seemed like defeat; but she would say
'Reculer pour mieux sauter,'
The future Henry II   Dandling young Henry on her knee,
And chuckling what a king he'd be!

Her little Henry quickly grew,
And by a brilliant piece of woo
1152   He married Eleanor, once queen
Of France (she 30, he 19).
Geoffrey had died the year before,
So all was his; now Eleanor
Brought Aquitaine into his grasp –
A realm to make all Europe gasp,

Especially since (too long to tell)
He lorded Brittany as well.
It therefore comes as no surprise
That England danced before his eyes.

In those days, major wars were fought,
Like any seasonable sport,
At quiet times upon the farm,
When lack of hands would do least harm
(Excluding winter, when no one
Would find outdoor pursuits much fun).
So when, against all tact and reason,
Young Henry landed out of season,
King Stephen had to go and get
His lads out in the cold and wet.
They found themselves some drier bits,
Banged a few heads, and called it quits. Wallingford 1153

In conference at Winchester,
King Stephen promised to confer
The crown on Henry, as his heir.
Just about everyone was there,
Anxious to be seen, and to show
They couldn't wait for Steve to go.
He took the hint: less than a year
Saw him laid out upon his bier,
And Henry crowned without delay.
We're told it was a joyous day.
'The king is dead – long live the king!'
What would our future fortunes bring?

House of Anjou (The Plantagenets) 1154—1399

The shrub *planta genista* grew
In unsprayed farmland in Anjou:
And since Count Geoffrey liked to pluck
A buttonhole, its name has stuck.
Though possibly not quite as keen
On ladies as Will's sons had been,
Their moods, most sudden and frenetic,
Might now be called plantagenetic –
King Henry was inclined to fits
Of screaming, pulling things to bits,
And wrecking all the royal beds
By tearing mattresses to shreds.

Yellow broom

Henry II 1154–89

Although things went to pieces later,
He was a good administrator,
And kept his empire in order,
From Ireland to the Spanish border,
By going ceaselessly about
And sorting any trouble out.
The first time in our history
A crowned king crossed the Irish Sea
Was when King Henry took a fleet
To see what forces they would meet.
Some chieftains chatted in the rain:
He shook hands and went home again.

Visit to Ireland 1171–2

Made Archbishop of
Canterbury 1162

The error that would really stick
Was over the Archbishopric.
His good friend Thomas Becket, who
Was quite laid-back, and well-to-do,
Gained quick promotion, till he swore
To serve the king as Chancellor.
Meanwhile, the Church and State were split,
And Henry was fed up with it;
So he got Becket to agree
To head the kingdom's Primal See.
With Thomas carrying the cross
He'd show those bishops who was boss!

Poor Henry must have been appalled
Once worldly Thomas was installed.
His habits now became less nice:
He wore a hair shirt stiff with lice,
And his whole creed was so unbending,
The two men's friendship cracked past
    mending.
Thinking a legal judgement flawed,
Disgusted Thomas went abroad,   1164–70
And talked of closing every church –
Leaving salvation in the lurch.
Faced with this, harassed Henry said:
'I wish the wretched man were dead.'

41

It seems unlikely that he meant
To have that armoured party sent
Across the Channel on the ferry

Becket's martyrdom
29 Dec 1170

And to the church at Canterbury.
No murder should, of course, disgrace
The precincts of a holy place;
But Thomas wouldn't go outside
Regardless of how hard they tried
To make him take a breath of air,
And so they killed him then and there.
The townsfolk came to shed their tears –
And snip his clothes for souvenirs.

Although to some he was a tartar,
Most thought of Becket as a martyr:
No sooner had he been interred
Than signs and miracles occurred,
Which all who benefited thought
His saintly spirit must have wrought.
(In absolutely record time
The Pope declared his life sublime.)   1173
King Henry, counselled by his friends,
Set out barefoot to make amends,   Public penance 12 Jul 1174
And lie prostrate, be flogged, and pray
Where his old boon-companion lay.

43

Another thing that set him brooding
Was the interminable feuding
With his four sons, who, he had planned,

Henry, Richard, Geoffrey,
John

Would share the tenure of his land.
Some hope! Each brother wanted more;
For fifteen years they were at war
With Dad as well as with each other,
Egged on by their intriguing mother,
Queen Eleanor, whose court in France
Was famous for its song and dance.

For 16 years

He locked her up to get some peace:
But still the feuding didn't cease.

Two sons were dead, but he fought on
With Richard and the youngest, John.
Philip, the King of France, who saw
A useful outcome from this war,
Joined in: without a single friend,
King Henry knew it was the end.

At Chinon 6 Jul 1189

In sickness and despair, he died:
But when Prince Richard stood beside
The royal corpse, at Fontevrault,
Its nostrils suddenly let flow
A stream of blood, as if to say:
'You get up my nose. Go away!'

RICHARD I 1189–99

King Richard's undistinguished reign
Was one continuous campaign
Against his Continental foes:
How we kept going, goodness knows.
Known as the Lionheart, he went
To every single tournament –
Or, if it rained, he lazed indoors,
And listened to his troubadours.

1190

He charged off on the Third Crusade,
For which his English subjects paid,
But fetched up on a hostile shore:
His ransom cost a whole lot more.

While all this fuss was going on,
A thought occurred to brother John.
Richard, not trusting him an inch,
Had made him promise not to pinch
The throne: with Richard now immured,
Perhaps the crown *could* be secured?
John needed backing for his coup,
But Philip had some men who'd do
(Provided John would go to Paris
And wed his spinster sister Alice).
John plotted, raised rebellion's head –
Heard Richard was released, and fled.   1194

What was the French king's interest
In helping to foment unrest?
Well, though the nation's overlord,
His nobles held the sharper sword,
And found convenient excuses
To cancel pacts and forego truces.
So really, though he was the king,
He hardly governed anything,
And stayed shut up in his domain.
This, luckily, adjoined Champagne,
Whose product kept his cellar busy
(Though in those days it wasn't fizzy).

Thus, Philip saw a golden chance –
Richard and John owned half of France,
And if they went to war, their lands
Might fall into his waiting hands.
But Richard simply kissed his brother,
Put him in some desk job or other,
And hurried off again, to bar
The French king's push towards the Loire,
Where fruitful vineyards stand in rows,
And blushing Anjou Rosé flows.

The thought drove Philip half insane –
There's nothing worse than flat champagne.

And then – a bolt out of the blue.
A crossbow archer at Châlus,
Who hadn't dipped his shaft in Jeyes,
Abruptly ended Richard's days.   6 Apr 1199
As he faced agonizing death
From gangrene, with his dying breath
He named John as the king to be,   JOHN 1199–1216
Engendering controversy,
Since Arthur, brother Geoffrey's son,
Was widely thought to be the one.
John took his nephew into care:
He disappeared, we don't know where.

Since no one really trusted him,
John's governance was pretty grim.
In Ireland (his one success),   1210
His forces managed to suppress
The English lords who'd sallied forth
And built their castles in the north;
But Philip launched a two-year war,
And won the wine he thirsted for.   1214
All John had left was Aquitaine:
The barons started a campaign
Against his rule, and, as a starter,
Requested him to sign a Charter.

Signed 15 Jun 1215

Though Magna Carta's been around
So long, and has a hallowed sound,
Not much of it turns out to be
To do with Rights and Liberty
(Clause 35, for instance, states
We ought to unify our weights).
In any case, its sealing wax
Had hardly cooled before the cracks
Of civil strife were widening.
The barons rose against the king,
And even managed to persuade
The French prince, Louis, to invade.

The Dauphin, in that tongue of theirs
(Though this is rather splitting heirs),
Quickly took London: his success   May 1216
Left King John in a real mess.
From now on, as a safety measure,
He travelled with his royal treasure;
But when his wagons crossed the shore
Beside the Wash, the poor man saw   12 Oct 1216
The tide-swept quicksands overwhelm
The riches of his quaking realm.
The estuary of the Nene
Is where his jewels were last seen.

A fever sent him to his bed,
And in a few days he was dead.   Newark 18 Oct 1216
A local abbot, who had tried
To save him, cut out his inside
(To keep for relics, like a martyr's,
Or just to use his guts for garters?).
King Henry, nine years old, was named;   HENRY III 1216–72
And since the lad could not be blamed
For what had taken place before,
It took the sting out of the war.
They threw out Louis, made amends,
And everyone was best of friends.

To give the boy a helping hand
A regency now ruled the land.
Its leader, near three score and ten,
Forgotten now, was mighty then:

1147–1219 William the Marshal served the nation
Despite outrageous provocation.
(King John, though he recanted later,
Had called this faithful knight a traitor,
Taken his castles, seized his wares,
And held as hostage both his heirs.)
'I trust myself to God and you,'
Said Henry – or he's rumoured to.

At thirteen, he was crowned once more
(They'd just used odds and ends before),   1220
But Edward the Confessor's Abbey
Now looked embarrassingly shabby.
So he demolished it, and said:
'I'll build a proper church instead,
In lofty Gothic, where there's room
For every future monarch's tomb;
Where people in the first six rows
Can see by standing on their toes –
A place where cameras will flash,
And tourists spend loads of cash.'

Westminster Abbey begun
1245

Though good at building, Henry lost
Yet more of France, at mounting cost;
Though thankfully not even he
Could help retaining Gascony,
Whose claret wines began to flow
To Bristol from its port, Bordeaux.
His wasteful, autocratic reign
Upset the barons yet again.
They'd fought his Dad for his consent
To have their say in government –
They were no further to the fore,
And so they had another war.

Simon de Montfort was the head
Of their revolt; at Lewes he led

Battle of Lewes 14 May 1264   A brilliant fight, and seized the king.
But next year came the reckoning

Battle of Evesham   At Evesham, when in wind and rain
4 Aug 1265   Four thousand in two hours were slain.
Prince Edward, Henry's martial son,
With odds of three or four to one,
Flew rebel banners as he came –
A dirty way to play the game.
De Montfort's head was put on view,
His private parts included too.

At sixty-five, Henry retired –
Well, in plain language, he expired,
And Edward Longshanks, first of three,
Revitalized the monarchy,
Jumped on his horse with sword and shield,
And forced all foreigners to yield.
In fact he'd gone off on crusade
When Father's last respects were paid,
And hurried back to bring some order
To England's ill-defended border:
The Welsh and Scots, a threat of old,
Still wouldn't do what they were told.

EDWARD I 1272-1307

'Britannia' was this island's name
Way back, before the Romans came.
But though our colonizers found
The south and east receptive ground,
The rest, as far as they could see,
Was not at all their cup of tea.
A periodical foray
Had kept those wild folk at bay,
Although the Scottish realm had been
A monarchy since 1018,
And English rulers might export a
Particularly hardy daughter.

Malcolm II (Macbeth's grandfather)

King Edward, basically, was smitten
By visions of United Britain.
The time was ripe: his chests were full
Of silver from exported wool
(Nine hundred 'woolfells' – sheepskins –
        bound
For Europe, earned the King a pound).

Llywelyn ap Gruffydd
r. 1246–82
Treaty of Conway 1277

The Welsh prince, Llywelyn, had no choice,
And signed surrender; but his voice
Was strong in this melodious land,
And brother David led a band

1282

Of freedom fighters, whose revolt
Gave Edward a terrific jolt.

This time he didn't mess about:
He gave the Welsh a mighty clout,
And with Llywelyn's severed head
Declared their line of princes dead.
But in Caernarvon, by design
(Or so it seems), the next in line
Was born; and like all later males   Edward (II) b. 1284
Received the title *Prince of Wales*.
Ten castles, some of which still stand,
Rose up to dominate the land.
Royal Caernarvon was the best;
Odd barons made do with the rest.

His Scottish strategy had been
To wed his son to their young queen,
'The Maid of Norway', who then died
Aged seven. Luck stayed on his side,   Margaret (Scotland)
For since there was no other heir   r. 1286–90
The Scots were forced to look elsewhere,
And Edward, by long custom, came
To ratify the choice of name.
John Balliol, he thought, would be
A less determined enemy
Than Robert Bruce, so he put down
The luckless John to wear the crown.   John (Scotland) r. 1292–96

With such a king, Edward felt free
To march in with impunity,
Claim all the lowlands as his own,
1296   And force John off the Scottish throne.
We know what Robert Bruce then did:
He watched a patient arachnid
Construct its website, and although
It kept on crashing (don't we know?)
It went back to a re-design
Until it got itself on-line.
What was a mob of English thugs,
Compared with fixing all those bugs?

Inspidered, Robert Bruce became
The emblem of his country's name.
Robert I (Scotland) r. 1306–29   They seated him upon the throne
(Though Edward had removed the Stone
Of Scone, whose recent restitution
Acknowledged Scottish devolution).

Once William Wallace's attacks

Guerilla leader 1270–1305

Had undermined the Sassenachs,

The Scottish tide began to turn,

Till they broke through at Bannockburn.

23–24 Jun 1314

King Edward's son now wore the crown:

His rule turned England upside-down.

EDWARD II 1307–27

The barons' power, like a spring

Tight-wound, would threaten any king

Unwise enough to let it loose.

Edward the First had forced a truce,

But this new fellow liked to play

With male favourites all day,

And simply didn't see the sense

Of coming to their 'Parliaments' –

The barons' councils they were due

When Magna Carta was rushed through.

(Though still-born, its ideas lived on,

To nurture and to build upon.)

This catastrophic barons' war
Was worse than anything before,
Since bloody vengeance soon became
Unworthy Edward's only aim.
Their marital relations tense,
Queen Isabella had the sense
To flee to friendly France, and start a
Revolt with her inamorata
The ruthless Roger Mortimer.
London turned out to welcome her:
This puissant pair usurped the State
And made her husband abdicate.

Isabella & Mortimer 1327–30

Edward the Second disappeared:
Murdered, no doubt; and it is feared
A red-hot poker may have been
Inserted in his intestine.
His wife now queened it over all:
She and her henchman had a ball
Despatching subjects one by one,
Till her rebellious teenage son
Told her the party had to stop,
And gave her other half the chop.
Queen Isabella kept her head
And turned into a nun instead.

The third King Edward's reign was stable:
He even planned his own Round Table
Of fearless knights (with modest maids
Disarming them in sunlit glades);
Of plangent minstrelsy and song,
And feasts that went on far too long.
His wife Queen Philippa and he
Were overwhelmed with progeny,
Whose subsequent dynastic claim
Would give the Roses Wars their name.
But those rough times have not come yet:
The kings are still Plantagenet.

61

Though Edward's knights enjoyed their sport,
There were some battles to be fought.
With peace at home (apart, of course,
From Scotland, still restrained by force)
The country clamoured to unite
Behind a cause it felt was right.
The French gave Edward an excuse,
For Charles the Fourth could not produce
An heir, so Isabella's name
Gave England's king some sort of claim.
Main fighting 1340–60 · The Hundred Years War raged for twenty,
Treaty of Calais 1360 In which time Edward conquered plenty.

The knightly code did not apply
To base-born folk: they let them fry
In their own blaze, or chopped them down
Once they had overcome a town.
At Limoges, Black Prince Edward slew   Edward's heir
Three thousand of them – children too;   1370
Though gentle Philippa insisted,
When Calais fell, that they desisted.   1347
The name of Poitiers resounded   1356
At knightly tables, square and rounded:
The Black Prince captured France's king
And brought him back for ransoming.

But this war only hurt a few
Compared with what black rats could do:
They travelled from the east, and spread
The virus that left millions dead.
Malignant 'Acts of God' were thought
To mean bad marks on our report,
So when the Black Death swept the land   1349 onwards
The Day of Judgement seemed at hand.
It's likely that at least a third
Died in the years when it occurred.
Nobles in castles fared the best:
They'd obviously passed the test.

There was no cure: once caught, it killed.
In towns they dug huge pits, which filled
With corpses barnacled with sores,
Blood clogging their grimacing jaws,
Decaying to a jellied mess
Beneath the unrelenting press
Of next day's deaths: and with them fell
Their ministering priests as well.
(The 'Ring-a-ring-of-roses' rhyme,
Though made up in a later time,
Describes the fatal rash that spread
Until the sufferer was dead.)

The Black Prince, whom no lance could slay,
Picked up some bug and passed away   1376
Before his father; so his son,
Young Richard, was the chosen one,
Inheriting when ten years old.   RICHARD II 1377–99
He wasn't in his father's mould:
He had no taste for sword and axe,
And knights exchanging mighty whacks;
His nobles looked at him askance
When he promoted peace with France.
These good intentions were in vain:
He had a most unhappy reign.

At fourteen, though, he faced a test
That left his elders quite impressed.
Peasants' Revolt 1381
Revolting peasants, in a crowd
(Far more than safety regs allowed)
Led by Wat Tyler and Jack Straw,
Had thumbed their noses at the law,
And marched to London, to complain
At being poll-taxed yet again.
He said he'd see what could be done,
And hanged their leaders one by one –
Though it *was* scotched, as it would be
When introduced by Mrs T.

The smelly peasantry retired,
But scheming nobles were inspired
To gain control for their own ends,
'Merciless' Parliament 1388
And liquidated Richard's friends
Before he had sufficient clout
To stop them. When he wiped them out
Years later, in a well-planned coup,

Fears grew about what else he'd do.
His self-conceit had grown so high,
If anybody caught his eye
They had to kneel three times. In short,
He kept them pretty fit at Court.

The House of Lancaster now makes
Its entrance in the Royal Stakes,
For Richard's line was in a mess:
The nursery was childless.
A cousin, Henry Bolingbroke,

Son of John of Gaunt, Duke of Lancaster

Was fancied by the common folk,
So Richard had him sent away

Bolingbroke banished 1398

To take a six-year holiday,
And all his lands and goods were seized.
Henry was not exactly pleased.
He came back with sufficient backing

Landed at Ravenspur July 1399

To send short-sighted Richard packing.

Abdicated 30 Sep 1399

House of Lancaster 1399—1471

With Richard's fall, the Anjou line
Went into terminal decline,
And Lancaster was suddenly
The up-and-coming dynasty,
Though it endured some stormy weather,
With just three monarchs altogether.
Each was called Henry, Four to Six.

HENRY IV 1399–1413

The first (the Fourth) was keen to fix
The Scots and Welsh, and close their
                   borders:

Earls of Kent and Salisbury

But two of Richard's earls gave orders
To cook usurping Henry's goose
And set the rightful monarch loose.

Their plan was, as the record claims,
'Under the guise of Christmas games',
To cut off every royal head.

HO HO
HO

With hours to spare, their quarry fled,
While they themselves took headlong flight
For Cirencester. What a night!   5 Jan 1400
Decapitations, homes burned up –
You'd think the town had won the cup.
Soon after, Richard passed away:
Done in or starved we cannot say.
The only undisputed fact
Is that he died at Pontefract.

Henry was always insecure.
His dubious investiture
Nagged him; and soon he had to face
The Earl of March's claim, whose case   See p.78
Depended on his own descent
From Edward. Scheming March had sent
Proposals to the Welsh (whose power
Had re-emerged under Glendower),
And to the northern Percys, who
Had shown the Scots what they could do.   Battle of Homildon Hill 1402
They all decided that the king
Was overdue for toppling.

Henry beat down the Percys' forces
Battle of Shrewsbury 1403
At Shrewsbury; but men on horses
Had real problems in the hills
Against Glendower's combat skills.
He'd asked the French to come and share
Their barrels of *vin ordinaire,*
Which raised the Welsh to dizzy heights:
Joint siege 1404
They had Caernarvon in their sights!
Then York rebelled. Henry saw red,
Richard Scrope 1405
And cut off the Archbishop's head;
But felt bad, seeing what he'd done,
And quickly found another one.

So all in all, King Henry knew
He had a lot of work to do
Just hanging on to what he'd taken,
Recurrent strokes had left him shaken,

So he asked Henry, Prince of Wales,
To supplement his tele-sales
By giving him a helping hand.
Hal's wild exploits swept the land –
Which foes he'd slain, or forced to yield;
What he got up to off the field;
The pubs and clubs he liked the best;
His boozing pals… and all the rest.

King Henry saw this in *Ye Sunne*,
The paper read by everyone.
He groaned to Hal: 'Didn't I stress
The power of the tabloid press?
This says the common folk would rather
Have you for king – and I'm your father!'
'Don't worry, Pop,' young Henry said:
'I'll have a ball till you drop dead,
But once they've given me the crown,
I guarantee I'll settle down!'
(To read the verbal transcript, see
Henry IV Part I, Act III.)

HENRY V 1413–22

Henry the Fifth, it's fair to say,
Owes Shakespeare and Olivier
A debt of thanks for how they made
His reign a glorious cavalcade.
He used the time-worn argument
That France's throne should, by descent,
Belong to England, and therefore
We'd every right to go to war.
But did he also, shrewdly, see
That one external enemy
Would help our lacerations heal
Through new-born patriotic zeal?

At any rate, he sent a note   Mar 1415
To Charles the Sixth, from which I quote:
'Dread Sire, I demand your land
To rule as king; also the hand
Of Princess Katherine. Please sign
The treaty on the dotted line,
And pay the itemized account.
Yours, Henry.' Part of this amount
Was ransom they were meant to pay
After the Treaty of Calais,
Plus two million French crowns for Kate –
They offered him her going rate.

The French insulted him by sending
A chest of tennis balls, pretending
That he was simply playing games.
They soon perceived his real aims.

22 Sep 1415   He won Harfleur, a vital port;
But now the days were getting short,
And nobody, without good reason,
Would go on battling out of season.
So off they marched to catch the ferry,
Cold, wet and sick, and far from merry,
When, on the eve of Crispin's Day,
French horsemen barred their weary way.

Battle of Agincourt   How could so few beat down so many,
25 Oct 1415   And, by the end, lose hardly any?
The rout of Agincourt's explained
By (a) the fact that it had rained,
Which bogged the Frenchmen in the mud;
By (b), the diabolic thud
Of arrows hitting them; and (c)
Their leaders' lack of unity.
The English troops were told to slay
All fallen men, though they should pray
For mercy. Some six thousand died;
Two hundred-plus on Henry's side.

All London was delirious.
The lads rode in an open bus,
And Henry never would be short
Of honour after Agincourt.
The French king, utterly depressed,
Signed over all that he possessed   Treaty of Troyes 1420
To Henry, as his dubious heir,
At which the Dauphin (prince) went spare:
This gangster-king had pinched his land
And also won his sister's hand!
(Yes! Henry, who had had to wait
Five years, could now say 'Kiss me, Kate'.)

She held him for two years, no more:
This Henry was a meteor
Pulled down from the celestial sphere
By agonizing diarrhoea.
The kingdom fell upon his son,

HENRY VI 1422–61,
1470–71

Who at that time was not yet one:
But when he grew into the crown
Its golden burden weighed him down
(His queen's ambition pulled him through –
The ruthless Margaret of Anjou).
Henry the Sixth's shambolic reign
Plunged England into war again.

With Henry prematurely dead,
Our French exploits came to a head –
As happened many times before,
The country lost its taste for war
In foreign parts: we gained a bit,
Then struggled to hold on to it.
The French who, by the terms of Troyes,
Were governed by an English boy,
Soon blazed up, fired by the spark

The 'Maid of Orleans'
?1412–31

Struck in their hearts by Joan of Arc.
Were her transcendent voices real,
Or was it just her sex appeal?

Joan went around in men's attire:
The English sent her to the fire
To make it clear that, in their view,
Cross-dressing simply wouldn't do.
But even after she was gone,
Her charismatic flame burned on.
Les rosbif, overdone, retired,
And gave up all that they'd acquired
Apart from Calais; for this shame
The king was, naturally, to blame.
The Red Rose withered on its stalk;
From Lancaster they turned to York.

In Rouen
30 May 1431

English expelled by 1450

A complex network of descent
Led to the Roses Tournament.
Edward the Third had many sons:
His heir died; of the other ones,
John, Duke of Lancaster, had sown
Red roses round the English throne,
Producing Henrys, as we've seen.
But well before this, there had been
Another older son as well,
Who passed away, called Lionel.
He had a daughter, Philippa:
Things hotted up because of her.

i.e. Henry IV

If Philippa had been a male
No way could his (or her) claim fail,
Since he (or she) was next in line
When Richard died. But to assign
The throne to women was not on,
And so the honour fell upon
Henry of Lancaster instead.
But Philippa went on to wed
The Earl of March: the son she bore
See p.69 Would later, as I've told, make war
On Henry, since his mother's name
(He said) gave him a stronger claim.

If this is clear, it's time to talk
About the rival House of York.
Its duke was way down in the list
Of Edward's sons, so he had missed
All chance of ever being king.
But after some manoeuvring
His son was brought into a plan
With Philippa's grand-daughter Anne,
To merge two lines of royal rank
Within the York genetic bank.
This done, the White Rose and the Red
Were ready for the games ahead.

St Albans (north of Watford) hosted
The first match, when the White team coasted
To such an easy win, the Reds
Lost several distinguished heads.
Since Henry had a life contract
They didn't think he could be sacked;
The Duke of York, though, took the helm,
Named as Protector of the realm.
Queen Margaret, stuck with Henry, tried
To get new players on her side,
Driven by one resolve alone –
To get the Reds back on the throne.

Five years of skirmishes went by.
Then came the bloody Wakefield tie:
The Duke's head, plus a couple more,
Were stuck up high to show the score.
The rampant Reds went clamouring
Down to St Albans, where the king
Had been imprisoned, got him out,
And had another brilliant rout.

1st Battle of St Albans
22 May 1455

Battle of Wakefield
30 Dec 1460

2nd Battle of St Albans
17 Feb 1461

But since the stewards were concerned
The capital might end up burned
They held them back, to calm them down –
Amazed, the Whites marched into town.

Edward acclaimed 4 Mar 1461

Edward, the Duke of York's sole heir,

EDWARD IV 1461–70, 1471–83

Was tall and well-built, with an air
Of majesty poor Henry lacked.
He liked the ladies – that's a fact.
When he was crowned by acclamation
Margaret turned down his invitation
To drinks (although they'd love to stay,
They really had to dash away).
Edward, who liked to entertain,
Chased them to Towton, asked again.

Battle of Towton 29 Mar 1461

They had the best bash of the war:
Ten thousand died, or maybe more.

But Margaret did not give up
All hope of winning back the cup.
The kings of France, and Scotland too,
1470   Helped her to organize a coup
That brought bewildered Henry back
Until King Edward's last attack
Battle of Tewkesbury   At Tewkesbury. The whistle sounded:
4 May 1471   The Reds' equipment was impounded,
And Henry's further hopes of power
Were somewhat dented in the Tower –
His skull, preserved at Windsor, shows
The evidence of mighty blows.

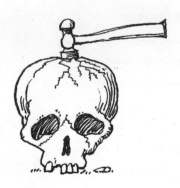

House of York 1461—85

King Edward had to raise some cash
To help his court to cut a dash.
He warred on France, and made them pay
Large sums to take his troops away,
Then put his brother George in clink
And gave him more than he could drink
(His sorrows drowned while upside-down,
His lands in forfeit to the crown).
Even Queen Margaret's ransom went
To help with the refurbishment.
His lifestyle, though, was most unhealthy:
He grew obese as well as wealthy.

Duke of Clarence
d. 18 Feb 1478

Like many other monarchs, Edward
Escorted lots of ladies bedward;
But when it came to marrying,
Right royal blood was everything.
So when they found him a princess
Who'd be a sure-fire success,
And heard he'd married on the quiet,
It practically caused a riot.
A daughter of that Woodville clan!

Elizabeth Grey ?1437–92   Widow of a *Lancastrian*!

What made the senseless fellow choose
From those rapacious parvenus?

The Woodvilles naturally saw
Potential in this son-in-law:
They picked up titles, lands and brides,
And lots of other things besides.
At forty, though, his wick burned through:
A most unhelpful thing to do,
Since little Edward, Prince of Wales,

EDWARD V Apr–Jun 1483   Was but a minnow among whales.

The Woodville faction could confound
The Yorkists, if they had him crowned:
A quick pre-emptive coronation
Would give them total domination.

To challenge them, the floundering State
Produced its toughest heavyweight
And greatest landowner – none other
Than Richard Gloucester, Edward's
     brother.
The idea was that he would see
Young Edward through the Regency;
But Richard's role is still a theme
To stir the groves of academe.
Did he have both his nephews killed
To get his royal aim fulfilled?
Or was he statesmanlike and kind,
And unforgivably maligned?

King Richard said he seized the crown
When rumour spread around the town
That Edward's marriage to his queen
Was bigamous. This had to mean

Edward and Richard
That their two sons were both unlawful.
The prospect (Richard said) was awful:
The wilful Woodvilles would declare
That little Edward *was* the heir,
And rush his coronation through.
Just contemplate what that would do!
So Richard did a noble thing

RICHARD III 1483–85
In taking on the job of king.

That, in a nutshell, is the way
Pro-Richard folk see him today,
But, on the whole, most academics
Are not convinced by their polemics,
And think that Richard, steeped in blood,
Swept to success on fortune's flood.
The 'bastard princes' were a ruse
He opportunely put to use;
And since the boys were in his charge,
Why were they never seen at large?
So Shakespeare's Richard still rampages
On countless videos and stages.

His bloody regime ran its course:
That cry 'My kingdom for a horse!'
At Bosworth, where they cut him down,
Left Henry Tudor with the crown.
His claim was marginal. His mother
Claimed kinship with a bastard brother
Of Henry Bolingbroke, which meant
He was of dubious descent;
But since his blood was sort of Red,
He chose a White rose for his bed.
Elizabeth of York would link
Both warring hues, and turn them Pink.

Battle of Bosworth 22 Aug 1485
HENRY VII 1485–1509

House of Tudor 1485—1603

1491–99

Henry the Seventh watched his back:
For years he feared a White attack.
A scam his enemies contrived
Claimed that one Yorkist prince survived
And was preparing to invade.
The star part of the prince was played
By Perkin Warbeck, who went round
Insisting *he* should have been crowned
(His acting was so true to life
The Scottish king found him a wife).
This play's long run did rather well
Till Henry clapped him – in a cell.

Henry conceived a British realm,
With his son Arthur at the helm
And rival barons cleared away –
For that's where his main challenge lay.
Conveniently, the Roses war
Left fewer nobles than before:
He pinched the lands of those remaining,
And got the population training
With bows and arrows, spears or sticks
In case the French began their tricks.

88

He also had his private force:
The Yeomen of the Guard, of course.

Henry, a great administrator,
Would slave away till twelve or later.
He was distraught when Arthur died,
But widowed Katherine, a bride   Katherine of Aragon 1485–1536
Designed to foster links with Spain,
Was instantly espoused again
To Arthur's brother Henry, who   HENRY VIII 1509–47
Would need six wives to see him through.
He had a most frustrating wait
Before the Pope allowed him Kate
(The reason there was such a fuss
Is set out in Leviticus).   Levit. 18:16

89

Unlike his father, he'd no taste
For admin – it seemed such a waste
To spend time tracking down odd pence
Instead of fighting tournaments,
Or making Scottish raiders yield

Battle of Flodden 9 Sep 1513 (Most notably at Flodden Field).
That's why the place was really run

Chancellor 1515–29 By Wolsey, who was Number One
For fourteen years. But Henry's cares
Were centred on his lack of heirs.

Mary b. 1516 Mary was Kate's sole contribution –
Would Anne Boleyn be the solution?

Since Wolsey couldn't make the Pope
Annul Kate's marriage, Henry's hope
Of getting hold of Miss Boleyn
As queen, appeared extremely thin

Archbishop of Canterbury Till Cranmer very kindly judged
1533–53 The Pope confused, Kate's marriage fudged.
The docile statesmen stood in line

Act of Succession 1534 To read the judgement, swear, and sign;
But Henry clashed with Thomas More,
The man whom he'd made Chancellor.
When doubting Thomas shook his head,

Thomas More 1478–1535 They had to take it off instead.

For Henry, fixing the succession
Would be a positive obsession:
His urge to leave a male heir
Shattered the Church beyond repair.
Annulling Kate insulted Rome,
Ambassadors were sent back home,
And he was excommunicated.
The pregnant Anne, adorned and feted,
Soon gave birth – to another girl.   Elizabeth b. 1533
So now the axe began to whirl.
Anne's head flew off; then, to his joy,
His third wife, Jane, produced a boy.   Edward b. 1537

down with the pope

Though Henry got in such a mess
Over religion, he'd profess
The Catholic faith until he dropped.
The thing he really wanted stopped

Act of Supremacy 1534

Was papal rule. So, in this sense,
It is a mere coincidence
That European discontent

The Reformation

With what Catholicism meant
Should be already in the air.
Nor was he being doctrinaire
In closing monasteries down:
Their wealth was needed by the Crown.

King Henry's further wives did not
Increase his brood. Three was the lot:

The future Bloody Mary (who
When Father died was 32),
Elizabeth, the Virgin Queen
(The third in line, only 14),
And Edward, nine, a sickly child,   EDWARD VI 1547–53
Whose reign saw Protestants run wild.
The saint-crammed churches were stripped
    bare;
They used a Book of Common Prayer   First Prayer Book 1549
That dropped the Mass but kept the Creed;
And sold a Bible folk could read.   English Bible 1539

A thousand years had passed away
Since Roman faith arrived to stay.
Now all its tenets were taboo,
Plus Transubstantiation, too
(This meant that, when the Mass was said,
Jesus *became* the wine and bread).
No shrines, no effigies to handle –
They couldn't even light a candle.
But though some people did protest,
There wasn't general unrest,
Perhaps because the population
Was much more worried by inflation.

The silver in a coin, till then,
Had matched its token worth; but when
The bullion reserves ran short
They used less silver than they ought.
To people, silver was what counted –
So coins bought less, and prices mounted.
Landowners cursed: how could they find
More cash, when they were paid in kind
By muddy folk who owed no rent?

Enclosure Acts from late 15th C.

Unprofitable peasants went:
Their strips of land enclosed and green,
With more sheep than you've ever seen.

94

Hundreds of angry pickets met
At Norwich, led by Robert Ket,   Ket's rebellion 1549
Who helped to draft a bold petition
Explaining their unjust position.
John Dudley, Earl of Warwick, sent   Later Duke of
Some troops well-skilled in argument: Northumberland ?1502–53
This service gave his name a boost,
Inspired ambition, and unloosed
A grotesque scheme to undermine
The well-established Tudor line,
And get a Dudley on the throne
By machinations of his own.

Edward, now fifteen, had TB,
And Dudley got him to agree
To name Jane Grey, his cousin, heir
(Her wish was neither here nor there).
Arrangements had, of course, begun
For Jane to marry Dudley's son:
And once the pawn was queened and mated,
The Tudors would be subjugated.
King Edward died, and hapless Jane   JANE 10–19 Jul 1553
Commenced her 'Little Nine Days' reign:
All Mary Tudor had to do
Was show her face – and Jane was through.

BLOODY MARY 1553–58

Queen Mary liked her barbecues:
They all attracted hungry queues,
Though after the initial fun
The cooking did seem over-done.
Some say her father was to blame:
He'd disinherited her name
And spoiled her chances, as princess,
Of matrimonial success;
And then she had to hang around,
And see her baby brother crowned
And rip the Catholic church apart.
It wasn't a terrific start.

Two needs would dominate her reign:
Restore the Roman faith again,
And get an heir, to thwart her sister.
The one she banked on to assist her
Was Philip, king of Spain. A riot
Of protest, led by Thomas Wyatt,
Crashed to defeat on London's wall.   *Wyatt's rebellion 7–9 Feb 1554*
A hundred rebels hanged in all –
From which it can be recognized
That loyalties had polarized.
Still, Mary and her prince were wed,   *July 1554*
Though he was seldom in her bed.

To Philip, England was a tool
To strengthen European rule;
He started war with France, which cost

Calais surrendered to France
1558

The port of Calais; Mary lost
The only foetus she conceived
(Though she may well have been deceived),
And now, in deepening despair,
Saw heresy spread everywhere.

Bishops Latimer and Ridley
16 Oct 1555

As Latimer and Ridley waited
To be infernally cremated,
Latimer shouted to his friend:
'Our flame will burn until the end!'

After six years, the bloody tide
Retreated, for Queen Mary died

ELIZABETH I 1558–1603

And left Elizabeth the crown.
Another claim also came down
Through her Aunt Margaret, who'd gone north

James IV (Scotland)
r. 1488–1513

And married Scotland's James the Fourth.

Their son, the fifth James in succession,   James V (Scotland) r. 1513–42
Then left his realm in the possession
Of daughter Mary, Queen of Scots,   Mary (Scotland) r. 1542–67
Whose many years of plights and plots
And pleadings to be recognized
Would, after death, be realized.

Elizabeth could not forget
The fate her mother Anne had met
Through misplaced trust: right from the start,
She kept her inmost thoughts apart.
Her steadily improving skill
In hiding all her hand, until
She saw what suits her rivals held,
Was virtually unparalleled.
One special card she kept well back:
Herself, the strongest in the pack.
While monarchs thought they had a chance,
She'd be the one who made them dance.

To help her steer this leaky vessel

Later Lord Burghley 1520–98 She made good use of William Cecil,

Who stayed with her through thick and thin –

And what a mess the place was in!

Religious schism; coins debased;

The loss of Calais to be faced;

Unsettled peasants pinching bread;

Our export business almost dead;

Mary now Queen of France as well

(With French troops, Scotland might rebel):

How could the shattered State survive

Ruled by a lass of twenty-five?

Faith first. A balanced judgement saw

Both Churches could be argued for.

The clerics of the Reformation

Had sizzled in the conflagration,

And Rome restored could be a blessing.

But (though she kept her neighbours guessing

For some time yet) her Tudor head

Went for the other choice instead:

To keep her brother's church, and be

Act of Uniformity 1559 Unfettered by the Papacy.

She had endured her sister's reign:

She would not go that way again.

The next thing Bess attended to
Was finance. Over in Peru
Cheap cheerful folk dug silver ore
In quantities undreamt before,
So proper coinage, worth its weight,
Began once more to circulate.
Once this was done, it seemed unjust
That exporters were going bust –
But Antwerp, where most goods were sent,
Was Spain's; and now King Philip meant
To make things tough. The time was coming
When Francis Drake would start his drumming.

But Spain would gild her later days,
After a single giddy phase
That almost tore the realm apart.
Queen for two years, she lost her heart

Later Earl of Leicester
?1532–88

To Robert Dudley – mooned, lost weight,
Ignored the pressing needs of State,
And possibly (though it's not proved)
Planned how his wife might be removed.
This obstacle in their affairs

Amy Robsart d. 8 Sep 1560

Went head-first down a flight of stairs;
But now the road to bliss was clear,
Bess went right off the whole idea.

Through most of her tremendous reign
There ran the dominant refrain:
'Who will succeed her?' But she said
It was to England she was wed.
When she fell ill, and almost died,   Smallpox Oct 1562
Her councillors were petrified
(She should have got herself an heir:
It didn't matter how or where).
It all became a pointless cause
Once she had reached her menopause –
By which time everyone could see
The virtue of Virginity.

Ironically, she never met
The Queen of Scots, her greatest threat.
Half-French by birth, all French in manner,
She was the most upsetting spanner
In England's works. Mary's ambition
Was set on earning recognition;
But when, as France's widowed queen,

Landed at Leith 19 Aug 1561   She came to Scotland at eighteen,
She couldn't catch a word they said,
Which killed all conversation dead.
Communication was to be

'Marie' is how she spelled
her name.   A major problem for Marie.

Another problem was her height:
Six feet, when undressed for the night.
She married Darnley, inches taller,   Lord Darnley 1546–67
The first disaster to befall her –
To him, the whole thing was a game.
She tried to treat both teams the same
In Scotland's doctrinal divide,
But, naturally, the Papal side
Played her against John Knox, who preached   Calvinist reformer ?1512–72
Through faith alone is heaven reached.
He thought that dancing led to hell –
And Mary danced extremely well.

She had a hand, it's widely said,
In blowing Darnley up in bed   Kirk o'Field, Edinburgh
(The Casket Letters, tabloid stuff,   10 Feb 1567
Would later act as proof enough),
Then went off with her lover, who   Earl of Bothwell ?1535–78
Was known to have been in it too.
Now it was downhill all the way:
They took her realm and son away,
And rowed her out into a lake,   Lochleven Jun 1567–May 1568
Where she could ponder her mistake.
She wrote Elizabeth a note:
'Be with you soon – I've found a boat.'

The Virgin was perturbed indeed
On hearing Mary had been freed:
To have the next-in-line in tow
Was a worst-case scenario.
And so, to stop her escapades,

Imprisoned 1568–87 · She locked her up for two decades.
Though Mary claimed she was no threat,
A calculated trap was set:
A beer cask, she was made to think,
Could hold her post as well as drink,
So she and friends outside could plot:

Mary executed 8 Feb 1587 · The Barrel Letters caught the lot.

In Spain, widowed King Philip planned
How he might somehow win the hand

Of royal sister Number Two.
He saw his hopeful scheme fall through,
For England's queen would only mix
With other outlawed heretics.
Nor were his trading vessels free
From barefaced English piracy:
Bess said 'Well done!' when Francis Drake
Packed all the treasure he could take
Into the *Golden Hind*, and then
Sailed round the world and home again.   Circumnavigation 1577–80

107

So Philip, full of righteous ardour,
Assembled an immense Armada;
The Pope sent spiritual aid,
To what was really a crusade
To get the True Faith reinstated.
The re-vamped English navy waited
(And Drake played bowls), till Philip's force
Sailed up past Wight, and altered course
To land in Kent; but now the wind
Changed sides, and left the Spaniards pinned
On France's coast – a situation
With scope for active exploitation.

Battle of Gravelines
29 Jul 1588

108

The victory of Gravelines,
Apotheosis of the queen,
Gilded her reign; but, truth to tell,
Things were not going all that well:
Invasion still remained a threat,
And crops just rotted in the wet.   Famine 1594–98
Those new ships, plus the troops she sent
To fight Spain on the Continent
Meant taxes soared to pay the cost
(She recouped some of what was lost
By keeping up those useful trips
To unload Philip's treasure ships).   e.g. *Madre de Dios* 1592
                                                     (£80,000)

Not till her fifties did she make
Her one executive mistake:

1566–1601

She let young Robert Devereux,
The Earl of Essex, dazzle her.
She named him Master of the Horse
(Though she had more than one, of course),
And his exploits in foreign lands
Turned her to putty in his hands.
But when he glimpsed her half-undressed,
She had him put under arrest:
Incensed, he tried to stage a coup.

Essex rebellion 8 Feb 1601

It was the last thing he would do.

The jewelled lady in the ruff,

Elizabeth d. 24 Mar 1603

Eventually ran out of puff,
And with her sumptuous cortège
They laid to rest the Tudor age.
What was the secret of a reign
Whose like may never come again?
Surely because her rule expressed
The nation's soul. As she confessed:
'Though greater monarchs came before,
And there may yet be many more –
Of all this princely host, not one

Speech to Parliament
30 Nov 1601

Could love you more than I have done.'

House of Stuart 1603—1714

James VI (Scotland)
r. 1567–1625

King James, Queen Mary's son and heir,
Ruled Scotland when she left him there;
But not until his fourth decade
Was any declaration made
That he'd have England after Bess.
His mother's posthumous success
Was obviously the solution:
There was no whiff of revolution
When James the Sixth went south, to claim

JAMES I 1603–25

The realm in James the First's new name
(His second crown, it must be said,
Did go a little to his head).

King James' reign, as things turned out,
Was nothing to write home about;
But what an act to have to follow!
His cold disdain was hard to swallow,
And acid, carping argument
Embittered every Parliament.
He was inclined to fondle bits
Of current male favourites,
And spent a packet on his court,

Which had more power than it ought.
If he'd been blown up when he should,
It would have done his image good.

Sir Robert Catesby said he'd take
Four friends out to the Duck and Drake,
And buy them lunch, if they'd consent
To wipe out King and Parliament
And get the Catholics on top.
The project was a total flop,
Since it was leaked (some even say
It was *encouraged*, to betray
The greater number by its fall).
In fact, Guy Fawkes's part was small:
He had to set the fuse alight,
But really it was Catesby's Night.

Minor Catholic landowner
20 May 1604

Gunpowder Plot 5 Nov 1605

The first part of King James's reign
Saw peace at last agreed with Spain,
And he and Prince Charles hoped
    to catch
Spain's heiress in the Spanish Match
(Plus half a million pounds or more).

Thirty Years' War 1618–48   But Europe now flared up in war
As reigning Catholics attacked
Foolhardy monarchies that backed

War with Spain resumed 1624   The Protestants. The Match went out,
So Charles began to look about

Henrietta Maria 1609-69   In friendlier France, and made a hit –
Although her teeth stuck out a bit.

The Bible and King James's name
Are linked together by the fame

Authorized Version 1611   Of that stupendous new translation,
Which would be read throughout
    the nation.
In fact, he didn't like it much –
He thought it had a 'vulgar' touch,
Which tells us that those learned folk
Knew how the common people spoke
And laboured hard to reproduce
The language that was then in use.

114

The impact of its prose appears
Throughout the next three hundred years.

Since French and Latin had receded
As languages top people needed,
It was a most exciting time
For English, both in prose and rhyme.
The printing presses churned away,
Consuming forests, like today:
A sonnet, suitably recited,
Could get the coldest heart excited,
While playhouses (a new idea)   e.g. The Curtain 1577
Began to open up, and here
You'd find, all watching the same show,
The rich on high, the poor below.   The age of Shakespeare
                                           1564–1616

115

King James, it's said, liked nothing better
Than going off to the theatre;
But not all people could agree
That plays were healthy things to see.
Those killjoys, Puritans, were sure
That if you wanted to stay pure
You must shun pleasure and desire,
Or risk the everlasting fire –
Since sin could never be allayed,
Regardless of how hard you prayed.
So Puritans avoided plays,
And stayed indoors on holidays.

Elizabeth and James had each
Allowed the Puritans to preach;
But King Charles hated them on sight, CHARLES I 1625–49
Since his hope was to expedite
A change to a more Catholic way
Of worshipping from day to day.
Since Parliament mainly consisted
Of Puritans, who all resisted
Such 'Popery', both sides fell out.
His calls for money brought about
The final break. Charles told them flat:
'I'll rule without you – and that's that!' 1629

This sounds a radical solution.
Why wasn't there a revolution?
Well, Parliament could only sit
When monarchs had a use for it –
To raise the money for a war
Was usually what it was for.
But since Charles planned a peace with Spain
(Which meant no army to maintain),
He could, he hoped, reduce expense
And do away with Parliaments.
It worked all right until he made
The Scots conform in how *they* prayed. Scottish prayer book 1637

117

No way would this be tolerated!
As Presbyterians they hated
The bishops, bells and ballyhoo
That Anglicans were turning to.

Signed March 1638

A Covenant soon bound their nation
Against such 'Popish' innovation,
And to allay all further doubt
They went and got their soldiers out.
Charles couldn't fight (he had no men),

Treaty of Berwick 18 Jun 1639

So signed a truce, went home again,
And called a Parliament once more,

Short Parliament
13 Apr–5 May 1640

To stump up money for a war.

In session, he at once proceeded
To let them know how much he needed
To bash the Scots. He got a shock:
The MPs censured him *en bloc*
For what they saw as his abuse
Of power. Typically obtuse,
He kicked them out, scraped up a force,

Battle of Newburn 28 Aug
1640

And sent it north – it lost, of course.
The Covenanters got to York,
And after some high-level talk
They promised they would keep away.
The cost? £800 a day.

Completely broke, Charles had to call
His final Parliament of all –
It spanned the period that saw
The country plunged in Civil War.
MPs did not like confrontation;
They much preferred accommodation,
And would have met the king half-way
If he would let them have their say.
But Charles so polarized opinion
There was no hope of joint dominion:
He raised his flag, packed up his court,
And lived in Oxford while they fought.

Long Parliament 1640–53

Hostilities began 22 Aug
1642

119

1st civil war 1642–46

Five dark years followed, during which
The war hit both the poor and rich.
The issues lay so near the heart,
Whole families were split apart.
For monarchy or Parliament?
For Catholic or Protestant?
For England as she used to be,
Or some brave new society?
The Cavaliers (for Charles) were led

Charles's German nephew By bold Prince Rupert at their head;

The rebels (Roundheads) fought in groups –
But overall had far more troops.

Confusion over aims and means
Split Parliament behind the scenes.
Most wished Charles back, if he'd be good,
But doubted if he really would;
And Scotland said they'd help them fight,
But they must pray by Scottish rite,
And tolerate no other sect –
A change they promised to effect.
The writing now was on the wall,
For Rupert couldn't fight them all,
And Cromwell's charge at Naseby saw
The virtual ending of the war.

Solemn League & Covenant
1643

Battle of Naseby 14 Jun 1645

Oliver Cromwell 1599-1658

Cromwell, a prominent MP,
Was very good with cavalry,
And soon acquired the position
Of leading soldier-politician.
He wasn't happy with the way
The Scots were having so much say,
And worried where the church was heading,
With Presbyterianism spreading.
Nor, as the second-in-command,
Could he take Parliament's demand
To trim the Army once they'd won:
Another conflict had begun.

King Charles, though captive, held the key,
And could have saved the monarchy.
Both Parliament and Army tried
To get him signed up on their side,
Since he was still anointed king;
But he just stalled on everything.
Like grandmother, the Queen of Scots,
He had an appetite for plots,
And thought he could still win the war
And manage Parliament once more,
If Scotland sent its soldiers down
To help the forces of the crown.

Engagement with Scotland
Dec 1647

It must have been somewhat confusing   2nd civil war 1648
To find King Charles had started using
The Covenanters for support.
Cromwell, who up till then had thought
The king divine (although misled),
When he heard Charles's pact, saw red.
This was not war, but a crusade
Against a traitor who'd betrayed
God's trust! At Preston, Cromwell smashed
The Scots, and Charles's hopes were dashed: 17–20 Aug 1648
The Army now had total say,
And swept the monarchy away.   Charles I executed 30 Jan 1649

Declared 19 May 1649

And so the 'Commonwealth' began.
A self-selected Council ran
The day-to-day administration;

The Lords had been
abolished

The Commons passed all legislation.
Known as the Rump, it had no choice
Except to be the Council's voice,
Since opposition had been banned.
Religious fervour swept the land.

e.g. Massacre of Drogheda
11 Sep 1649

In Catholic Ireland, Cromwell slew
Whole populations, babies too –
For surely God was on their side
If He had sanctioned regicide?

This history is meant to be
A cheerful one; but I can't see
Much scope for entertaining rhyme
In that constrained and earnest time,
When any taint of fun or pleasure
Was thwarted, or bewailed at leisure.
Prince Charles, the heir, had fled abroad,
Till he was ripe to be restored.
He'd bring some colour to the face
Of England's pale populace,
And promise joyful times ahead –
At least, for those he took to bed.

The moment Father got the chop,
The Covenanters worked non-stop
To crown Prince Charles. As Scottish king
He'd be their puppet on a string,
Who would respond to every jerk
And back their missionary work.
He couldn't see what else to do
If he was to bring off a coup,
And swore away his Catholic soul

Charles' unholy covenant
3 Jul 1650

To Presbyterian control.
But then the English beat them hollow

Battle of Dunbar 3 Sep 1650

At Dunbar; worse things were to follow.

These setbacks gave them such a fright,
The Scots determined to unite
Against their enemy of old.
The Covenanters lost their hold,
And Charles was hustled off to Scone:

Charles II (Scotland)
r. 1651–85

His crowning took all afternoon
(I've no idea about the time –
I just said that to show the rhyme)
And then, quite sure that new supporters,
Plus lots of willing tapsters' daughters,
Would flock to him, he chose his steed,
Gathered his men, and crossed the Tweed.

Some hope! In fact, their ranks grew thinner.
In Worcester, where they stopped for dinner,
The troops of Cromwell had the sauce
To serve them up an extra course.

Battle of Worcester
3 Sep 1651

Charles got away, and spent six weeks
Enjoying many narrow squeaks
(Embellished in repeated versions)
And reached France after great exertions.
The Penderels, who gave him aid,
Still have a token pension paid
For letting him stay up a tree

Boscobel House,
nr Wolverhampton

(Since they did not do B &B).

So Prince Charles's coup was up the spout,
But Rump and Army soon fell out,
And Cromwell knew he had no choice
Except to be the country's voice.

Oliver Lord Protector 1653–58

And so, ennobled as Protector
(Although an influential sector
Wanted to see him crowned as king)
He tried to manage everything.
He did his best, that can be said;
But few mourned him when he was
    dead.

Richard Lord Protector
1658–59

Son Richard was a dismal flop:
The Commonwealth came to a stop.

29 May 1660

King Charles, restored, rode up
    Whitehall,

CHARLES II 1660–85

And London had itself a ball.
Our image of the Restoration
Is one of wild dissipation:
Of thigh boots, jingling spurs and plumes,
And badly ventilated rooms
Where willing wenches lie and wait,
And everybody gets up late.
But there's a wider panorama
Behind the lavish costume drama

Described in Pepys's Diary: Samuel Pepys 1633–1703
A spirit of *enquiry*.

Till then, it was believed and taught   e.g. at Oxford and
That all truth can be reached by thought.   Cambridge
The idea of Experiment
Was grotesque and irreverent:
For didn't holy scripture say
The world was fashioned in God's way,
And quite beyond our comprehension?
What He gave us was *apprehension*
Through which we were allowed to see
Our place in His cosmology.
Did we think we were God on high
To dare to question *How* and *Why*?

But in that fast-evolving era,
What we call 'science' came much nearer.

Galileo Galilei 1564–1642   When Galileo had the face

Dialogue 1632   To say the Earth revolves in space,
It gave religious folk a fright:
Did scripture really have it right?
From then, the human intellect
Became a scalpel, to dissect
The handiwork of the Creator;

Isaac Newton 1642–1727   And Newton showed, a little later,
That mathematics could apply

Principia 1687   To regions far beyond the sky.

Charles had the greatest sympathy
With 'Natural Philosophy';   Royal Society 1662
But more commercial problems pressed.
New colonies, to east and west   e.g. Virginia 1607
Were now maintained by sea, which made
The navy integral to trade:
If ships weren't where they thought they were,
Unforeseen problems could occur.
So Charles asked Wren if he'd design Christopher Wren 1632–1723
A splendid building, to define   Greenwich Observatory 1675
The line from which his sailors learnt
Just where they were (or where they weren't). Longitude 0°

King Charles, as happened much of late,
Inherited a bankrupt State,
And had to swear, and sign and seal
Many an undercover deal
Louis XIV r. 1643-1715 With Louis, Sun King, whose French francs
Shored up the breached Exchequer's banks.
These pacts arranged for mutual aid
Against the Dutch, whose sea-borne trade
And colonizing inclinations
Made them a nuisance to both nations;
But, in addition, Louis planned
Secret Treaty of Dover 1670 To see the Catholics rule this land.

This threat made Parliament promote
Test Act 1673 The Test Act, by a massive vote:
It said Top People had to be
Full members of the C of E.
The lack of any legal heir
(Though bastards frolicked everywhere –
A dozen figured in the list,
And I'll bet one or two were missed)
Would give the crown to brother James,
Whose unrepentant Roman aims
Charles blocked Exclusion Encouraged an attempted ban
Bill 1679 On monarchs who weren't Anglican.

This might have led to civil war,
As happened forty years before.
The good old diehard *Tories* banked
On heirdom being sacrosanct;
The *Whigs*, however, all agreed
That no new monarch should succeed
Without a measure of consent
Expressed by vote in Parliament.
A fabricated 'Popish Plot'   By Titus Oates 1649-1705
Had helped the Whig cause quite a lot;
But no one wanted to go through
Another 1642.

WITHOUT   WITH WHIG
                 SUPPORT

King Charles's reign is running out,
And I've not said a thing about
The Plague, the Fire, or Nell Gwynn!
Plague, as we've seen, was first brought in

See pp.63–64

By rats from the unhealthy East;
Once here, it never really ceased.

London, Mar–Dec 1665

The Great Plague, though, was much the
          worst,
And since it meant the realm was cursed,
The guardians of public care
Decreed bactericidal prayer:
If this did not prevent infection,
They left their dead out for collection.

The crowded houses of those days
Were often merrily ablaze
(A groom, getting his pipe alight,
Burned half of Newmarket one night);   22 Mar 1683
And if there was no water near,
The firemen made do with beer.
When London burned itself away,   Fire started 2 Sep 1666
They couldn't do much else but pray
As flames enveloped old St Paul's
And lead poured down in waterfalls;
While Pepys, a horrified spectator,
Saw smoke still rising six months later.   *Diary* 16 Mar 1667

Charles always found the time to go
To see the latest West End show.
He didn't care about the plot;
He simply went to talent-spot.

Waitress, orange seller
1650–87

Nell Gwynn had had a shaky start
Before she won the leading part,
But though she was just one of many,

They met c. 1668

It's said she loved Charles more than any.
Pepys called her 'Pretty, witty Nell'.
She had an impish side as well:
One night she worked out how to give
Charles's current mate a laxative.

When Charles was dying in his bed
He called his brother James, and said:
'Look after Nelly when I'm gone.'
The two men, though, had not got on.
Unlike the Merry Monarch, James   JAMES II 1685–88
Did not disguise his Catholic aims:
The Duke of Monmouth, Charles's son,
Rebelled, but James's army won.   Battle of Sedgemoor
                                                   5–6 Jul 1685
Two hundred hanged, when they were brought
Before Judge Jeffreys' famous court,   'Bloody Assizes'
While it took five inexpert hacks
To part the Duke's head with an axe.

King James soon lost the people's backing,
For he was noticeably lacking
In any sort of balanced view
Of what he might or might not do.
He had, he thought, God-given might –
So everything he did was right.
He soon gave Catholics commissions,
And put them in well-paid positions
In Government, and in the shires
(Which irritated Tory squires).
The Test Act's terms were still in force,
But he ignored all those, of course.

To overthrow the reigning king
Was not considered quite the thing;

'William of Orange' But William of the Netherlands
Would keep the crown in Stuart hands.
His claim was strengthened even more
By being James's son-in-law
(When he chose Mary as his Queen
She was still single at 15).
Will's enemy, Louis Quatorze,
Was threatening destructive wars,
And James's choice was clear to see:

First secret negotiations He'd fight for Faith, not Family.
Jan 1687

All were resolved; but even so,
A military overthrow
By, in effect, a foreign force,
Wrenched consciences. The fateful course
Was set when they heard James declare

'James III' b. 10 Jun 1688 His queen had borne a son and heir.
But William's fleet was hard to steer;
Mid-course, the wind began to veer,
Blew them past Yorkshire (where he meant
To land his army), right round Kent,
And puffed them west into Torbay –

5 Nov 1688 A good two hundred miles away.

138

This cock-up, though, appeared to be
A masterpiece of strategy.
The wind trapped James's fleet in port,
And since his spies and agents thought
A north-based coup would be attempted,
The rest of England had been emptied
Of royal troops. It's not clear whether
King James *was* beaten by the weather;
But, seeing that he had no chance,
He packed his bags and left for France.
All London hailed the royal pair,   18 Dec 1688
Despite Will's rather snooty air.   WILLIAM AND MARY
                                                         1688–1702

Though Parliament now rallied round,
They weren't sure how to get them crowned.
If James had only penned a line
That said 'It's all yours – I resign,'
(In other words, he'd abdicated),
The throne would then have been vacated;
But by strict principles of law
He still reigned, as he had before.
Some wanted the new pair to be
The rulers in a Regency.
They argued, then gave James the sack,   By vote in Parliament
In case he plotted to come back.   6 Feb 1689

139

Revivified by French cuisine,
James realized what a wimp he'd been;
So, with King Louis' troops, he planned
To raise a force in Ireland.

Irish Act of Recognition 1689

In Dublin, crowned by acclamation,
He urged that discontented nation
To fight the English occupier
With musket, pike and cannon fire.
At Londonderry, French troops tried

Siege of Londonderry
Apr–Jul 1689

To starve out everyone inside:
The few survivors of the slaughter
Drank horses' blood instead of water.

To William, Ireland was a bore,

Nine Years' War 1689-97

Distracting him from Europe's war;
But if James and the Jacobites
(As they were called) kept winning fights,
Then, as anointed king, he'd be
A focus for insurgency.
Resourceful William sent away
For foreign troops who'd like to play
Some practice games – they seized this chance
Of warming up to take on France.

Battle of the Boyne 1 Jul 1690

With his own Orangemen, he sent
'King James' into retirement.

With Ireland once more subdued,
King William could resume his feud
With Louis, whose determination
On European domination
Had forced his neighbours to declare
A Grand Alliance. This was where
The king and Parliament diverged
On aims: why should we get submerged
In all this Continental fuss?
Just what had Europe done for us?
Belligerency never paid:
Wars were disastrous for trade.

Treaty of Limerick 1691

German states, Holland,
Savoy and Spain

141

The Bank of England, which fulfils
The country's need to pay its bills,

Opened for
business
21 Jun 1694

Was founded now, to help advance
The cash for things like fights with France.
New customers were so impressed
To see a rate of interest
Of 8%, they fought like mad

Immediate
deposits £1.2m

To give it all the gold they had.
This money, in its turn, was lent
At profit to the government –
Which, ever since the scheme was born,

Origin of the National Debt

Has been sublimely overdrawn.

William and Mary's reign had been,
In practice, William's; for the queen
Had no administrative say.
Whenever he was called away
(Which happened often), all
    she'd do
Was sign things where they told
    her to.

Queen Mary d. 28 Dec 1694

But when this gentle lady died,
Her loss was felt on every side,
For as the undisputed heir
She'd been a *cordon sanitaire*

142

Between her husband and the men
Who wanted James brought back again.

e.g. Fenwick plot Feb 1696

The Allies won the Nine Years' War:

Treaty of Ryswick 1697

But what the hell had it been for?
Some forty millions had been spent
In battles on the Continent
Because the wretched man was Dutch!
The two sides disagreed so much
That William almost packed and went:
So now the Act of Settlement

Act of Settlement 1701

Was passed, in order to define
A sensible monarchic line.
It also put a total ban
On any who weren't Anglican.

A law which still applies today

QUEEN ANNE 1702–14

Anne, Mary's sister, took the throne.
Though married, she would rule alone
(Her consort, Denmark's prince, turned out
To be a royal lager-lout,
Unlike his sober forebear, who
Spent hours puzzling things through).
Nor did the product of her womb
Delight her, for it was the tomb
Of sixteen souls – or their brief share
Of life before our killing air.

William, Duke of Gloucester
1689–1700

The one who did survive his birth
Was still a child when laid in earth.

A single struggle dogged her reign:
To stop France getting hold of Spain.

S. America, W. Indies, Italy,
Belgium etc.

The Spanish empire was greater
Than any seen until much later,

Charles II, d. Nov 1700

And Charles, its dying king, expressed
A wish to leave all he possessed
To Sun King Louis' grandson, who
Was Prince of our old friend Anjou.
Both crowns united as one nation
Would be a fearful combination:

The Allies mustered ships and men
And staggered off to war again.

War of the Spanish
Succession 1702–13

The brilliant Duke of Marlborough led
The English forces, but in bed
He called surrender. War appealed
Far more than his own battlefield,
Where Sarah made his life a hell,
And dominated Anne as well.
Blenheim, his quintessential fight
Earned him a royal building site,
Where Vanbrugh became resigned
To Sarah's endless change of mind.
The Duke kept well out of the way,
Preferring camping any day.

John Churchill 1650–1722

Duchess of Marlborough
1660–1744

Battle of Blenheim
13 Aug 1704

Sir John Vanbrugh 1664–1726

While wanting France and Spain
    divided,
The English had by now decided
To merge with Scotland, a supporter

'James III'   Of James, 'the king over the water'.
If he returned to Scotland's shore
He'd bring the French, and start a war.
The Scots were happy to partake
Of England's economic cake,
And liked the thought of being freed
From customs duties at the Tweed:
But they would evermore resent

Act of Union 1707 created   The loss of their own Parliament.
Great Britain

In Europe, Louis' hopes were wrecked.

1713   He signed the Treaty of Utrecht
With Britain: we did not confer
With our great partner, Austria,
And picked up far more of the share
Than other Allies thought was fair.

e.g. Nova Scotia, Hudson's   Both France and Spain gave up
Bay, Newfoundland,   possessions,
Gibraltar   As well as valuable concessions
(Including one that really paid:
Suppliers to the Slaving Trade).

And since so much now went by boat
We had the finest fleet afloat.

The House of Stuart's regnal span,
From James the First until Queen Anne
(Eleventy-one years in all),   III by Hobbit numeralogy
Saw civil war, and monarchs fall.
But with its passing, there would be
Comparative tranquillity.
The soil was so well tilled and weeded
It grew more produce than was needed –
And this was what, in essence, led
To factories and urban spread:
For hands that hoed would now begin
To shape the age we're living in.

House of Hanover 1714—1901

Why Hanover? you'll want to know.
Surely we didn't have to go
As far as that to find a king?
Well, when they did the reckoning

1701 (p.143) That framed the Act of Settlement,
The only really safe descent

Elizabeth Stuart 1596–1662 Was through Elizabeth, the sister
Of Charles the First. Succession missed her,
But now the stunted Stuart vine
Produced fresh growth within her line:

GEORGE I 1714–27 So that's why George, her grandson, found
The Brits prepared to have him crowned.

George governed Hanover, a State

Elector of Hanover 1698

Within a great conglomerate –
The shrunken Holy Roman Empire,
Which would eventually acquire
The name and might of Germany.

1871 (p.188)

Despite his perfect pedigree
The Tories and the Jacobites,
Who backed the Old Pretender's rights,

i.e. 'James III'

Protested at this foreign king
With street parades and rioting.

Riot Act 1715

(It didn't matter if George heard –
He couldn't understand a word.)

King George, like William, had no use
For Parliament. It seemed obtuse
To have a king who couldn't do
Exactly what he wanted to:
In Europe there was no dispute,
Since monarchs there were absolute!
The answer was to choose MPs
Who would be very keen to please
(And see them voted to their seat
By covert threat, or perquisite);
And once all that was done, to get
The right men in his Cabinet.

Approx. 200 voters per MP
in 1760

149

It's at this point that we begin
To name the period we're in
According to the politician
Who occupies the Top Position.
This was Sir Robert Walpole's time:

Held office 1721–42 First minister, though not yet Prime.
Oct 1720 A scam, known as the South Sea Bubble,
Got small investors into trouble,
Although its backers had unloaded
Their shares before the thing exploded.
Sir Robert kept the hounds at bay:
They thanked him in the usual way.

The time of Walpole saw the rise
Of capitalist enterprise,
Encouraged by reforms he made
To help all those engaged in trade.
Since rural poverty had spread
(Due to enclosures, as I've said)
The booming towns were swelled by mobs
Of rowdy rustics after jobs.
Ten people sleeping on one floor;
Three babies dying out of four;
All sweetened by the heady scent
Of everybody's excrement.

It was the products of the loom
That underpinned the Georgian boom.
By crossing woolly sheep and rams
They turned out even woollier lambs;
And what with cotton coming in,

From the American colonies

They had far more than they could spin.
So treadles clanked and fingers bled
To keep the looms supplied with thread,
And bobbins bobbed, and shuttles flew.

John Kay's Flying Shuttle
loom 1733

Whole families, young children too,
Would slave while daylight let them see
At this new cottage industry.

With all this business going on
They still had to rely upon
The roads the Romans left behind,
By now completely undermined:
In less than favourable weather
Some brave souls vanished altogether.
Each parish spent a week a year
(In theory) keeping its part clear;
But since the locals rarely went
Beyond their farthest fields' extent,
Why should they throw their time away?
Let those who used the damned things pay!

Though roads were, as the crow flew, shorter,
Most people, wisely, went by water:

No gangs of highwaymen to fear,
And usable throughout the year
Except when winter's breath congealed
Its marble glaze on stream and field.   'Little Ice Age' c. 1450–1850
That's why canal-building began,
To take freight where no rivers ran.
But roads got better everywhere   Turnpike Acts started c. 1700
Once turnpike trusts began to share
Their costs and upkeep, by a charge
Anticipating *Le Péage*.   French motorway toll

CROP ROTATION

'Turnip' Townshend
1674–1738

Slum-dwellers with no bed or loo;
Piece-workers with too much to do…
They were the flotsam on the shore
As landlords fenced in more and more.
But some of these estates would show
The way all farming was to go.
For instance, root crops helped to feed
The soil for its future need;
While they kept cattle ticking over
Until next season's grass and clover –
Which came as a distinct relief
To those not keen on salted beef.

The reigns of Georges First and Second
Are very generally reckoned
The overture to what would be
The Iron Age of Industry.
But Commerce would bring war again

GEORGE II 1727–60

Halfway through George the Second's reign.

Louis XV r. 1715–74

The French, now ruled by Louis Quinze,
Were gaining rather useful lands
In Canada, and India too,
So action was long overdue;
And Spain maintained a constant raid

Export of negroes to W. Indies

Upon our buoyant slaving trade.

154

But France was also threatening
The safety of the British king,
For Louis was a staunch defender
Of 'James the Third', the Old Pretender.
Invasion forces at Dunkirk   Feb 1744
Were blown back, so that didn't work.
And then his heir, The Bonnie Prince,   Charles Edward Stuart
The stuff of legend ever since,   1720–88
Collected hordes of Highland men,
Whose massacre at Culloden   Battle of Culloden Moor
Preceded the extermination   16 Apr 1746
Of the remaining Gaelic nation.

The years till 1763
Saw Britain's navy all at sea,

e.g. Bengal 1757, Quebec 1759, Montreal 1760

Involved in daring expeditions
To snaffle France's acquisitions.
But Europe, too, was in a state

Frederick II of Prussia r. 1740–86

Because of Frederick the Great,
Whose ruthless Prussian musketeers
Were goose-stepping through frontiers
(Who knows where *they* would all have gone,
But for that man Napoleon?).
And so the Seven Years' War began –

1756–63

Which was, in fact, how long it ran.

The thought of combat mortified
Pacific Walpole, so he died.   1745
That great colonial, William Pitt,   Later Earl of Chatham
Became the driver for a bit –   1708–78
Or, to pursue the metaphor,
Stoked up the engines of the war.
Impossible to have about,
Impossible to do without,
George hated him, but had no choice –
His mood expressed the country's voice
(Though others, more adroit than he,
Looked after the diplomacy).

The French home fleet had been destroyed;   Off Lagos & Quiberon 1759
But Pitt was hardly overjoyed.
We'd got all Canada – that's true;   Treaty of Paris 1763
And they'd play ball in India too;
But it was utterly insane
To give them back their sugar cane;   Guadeloupe & Martinique
And as for getting a free hand
To trawl for cod off Newfoundland…!
The Paris treaty seemed a slight
On allies we'd left in the fight:
The Prussian king kept going on
About 'le perfide Albion'.

GEORGE III 1760–1820

Our new king, George the Third,
would manage
To do considerable damage
To what was now a buoyant nation
By changing the administration.
His father Frederick (the son
Of George the Second) had begun
To gloat at how he would replace
The Whigs' complacent power base
By docile Tories, who would do
Exactly what he wanted to.
A fit of coughing left him dead –
We almost had a king called Fred.

To fix what doesn't need repair
Is dangerously doctrinaire;
And toes were trod and feathers ruffled

Six first ministers 1762–70

As George (or Father's ghost)
reshuffled
His hotch-potch of a government,
And civil servants came and went.
The British empire was gigantic –
It even crossed the North Atlantic,
Where thirteen colonies now lay

Georgia the 13th colony 1732

From Georgia to Hudson's Bay.

(New Holland, south of the equator,
Would turn out very useful later.)

James Cook 1728–79 charted
Australia 1770

These colonies across the sea
Helped prop up the economy;
But their relationship to us
Was tricky and ambiguous.
They were the latest generation
Of migrants who, in desperation
(Too little owned, or too much owing),
Decided that they'd best be going,
Sold everything of any use,
And suffered weeks of lemon juice,
Foul food, and inefficient loos,
To shake our dust from off their shoes.

Through punitive restraint of trade
The British government had made
A splendid haul, since it controlled
The prices for which goods were sold
(The colonies, which it had bled,

$ not £

Were now nine million in the red).

Stamp Act 1765 (tax on
newspapers etc.)

The crunch point was a novel tax
To pay for fighting off attacks
By Indians, who couldn't learn
That it was now the white man's turn.
This started the disintegration:
'No tax without representation!'

Their problems found a ready ear
Once news had filtered over here,
For we were entering an age
When Liberty took centre stage.

'Liberté, égalité, fraternité'

The agitator Wilkes had fought
The government in open court,

*John Wilkes MP and
journalist 1727–97*

Which ruled (as he and others swore)
The State was not above the law.
Since no one seemed to have a clue,
George thought he'd see what Pitt could do:

First minister 1766–68

But William sat in private gloom
In Hampstead, in a darkened room.

The colonists refused to pay,
And so we tried another way,
Slapping a charge on every chest
Of tea – I'm sure you know the rest!

Boston Tea Party 16 Dec 1773

It was, quite likely, liquidated
To keep the smuggled price inflated;
But since they drank so much of it,
The Boston ladies had a fit
When all those tea-leaves went to waste.

c. 300 chests

Those rebels had no sense of taste!
(They could have sold it on the quay:
Buy one chest, get another free.)

First minister 1770–82

Troops deployed 1774

Lord North, when told about the loss,
Set out to teach them who was boss:
(And also show his strength of mind
To Wilkes and others of his kind).
His military subjugation
Helped forge the embryonic nation:
King George the Third can go to hell,
And take his troops with him as well;

Resolutions of Philadelphia
Congress 1774

The Brits won't get another cent!
We smiled, quite certain what this meant...
No banks or business acumen –
They'd soon be crawling back again!

4 Jul 1776

The Independence Declaration
Did not gain total approbation,

George Washington
1732–99

And Washington had quite a fight
To keep rebellion's torch alight.

General Burgoyne
surrendered
Oct 1777

But Saratoga's shock defeat
Made Britain realize that its fleet
Could not support this distant war
(We should have thought of that before).
The French, aware of our distress,

1778

Attacked us too, with such success
That Spain and Holland thought 'Why not?'
So now we had to face that lot.

The Versailles Treaty signed away

The newly-founded USA;

But though our realm was whittled down,

That Indian jewel in our crown,

Which I've disgracefully neglected,

Was relatively unaffected.

Its Tudor Company, state-aided,

Had long and profitably traded

In tea, silk, calico and cotton

(Plus other goodies I've forgotten)

Investors feeling well content

With dividends of 8%.

Once India split into states

With their aggressive potentates,

The Company was most impressed

At how the French (who then possessed

Substantial trading interests too)

Had quickly realized what to do.

They offered 'technical assistance'

For palace coups, or armed resistance –

Whichever seemed the better bet.

To counteract this growing threat

The British sent out arms and men:

So we were fighting France again.

1783

East India Company
founded 1600

Death of Emperor
Aurangzeb 1707

e.g. seizure of Madras 1746

Indian struggle 1744–61

The hard-pressed Company's survival
Was mainly due to the arrival

'Clive of India' 1725–74   Of an employee, Robert Clive,
Who couldn't stand the nine-to-five,
Attempted suicide but missed,
And thought he might as well enlist
And end it all while being paid.
He led a most revengeful raid
When Indians showed lack of feeling
By stuffing soldiers to the ceiling
Inside a cell – the famed Black Hole:

Black Hole of Calcutta   A kind of human casserole.
June 1756

Clive annexed parts; but Britain meant
To grasp the whole sub-continent,
And bloody was this final phase.

Under Richard Wellesley
Governor 1797–1805

Meanwhile, in France, the Marseillaise
Announced the downfall of its kings –

Bastille stormed 14 Jul 1789

A step, they hoped, to better things.
To supplement the guillotine
They'd redesigned their war machine,
Which undermined and overawed
All Britain's baffled friends abroad.

General offensive started 1793

In four years, from a standing start,
Europe belonged to Bonaparte.

Napoleon Bonaparte
1769–1821

This was the age of Pitt the Younger:
Emphatically no warmonger,

Chatham's son William,
1759–1806, made Prime
Minister at 24

Who damned electoral reform
And thought Free Trade should be the norm.
He didn't think it helped us much
To send troops to support the Dutch
(And he was right – it *was* a waste).
So eastward exploits were replaced
By a West Indian campaign
To seize all France's sugar cane.
They liked their coffee nice and sweet –
Without it, they would face defeat.

It was a bad time to decide
That being flogged until you died,
Plus maggots swimming in your gravy,
Could really turn you off the Navy.

Mutinies at Spithead and the Nore 1797

A few were hanged, or walked the plank:
The rest were whipped to sea, and sank

Battle of Camperdown 11 Oct 1797

A North Sea force, which Boney thought
Would finish us. Then Nelson caught

1 Aug 1798

His main fleet off the Nile delta,
And sent them gybing helter-skelter:

Horatio Nelson 1758–1805

Which made us master of the Med,

Emma Hamilton 1765–1815

And got him into Emma's bed.

This was, for those days, global war.
It hit all trade, made prices soar,
And what with rotten harvests too,
It's quite amazing we came through.
The starving poor were everywhere;

Introduced 1798

The rich thought Income Tax unfair;

Both sides, now knackered, felt it best
To sign a peace and have a rest.   Treaty of Amiens 1802
The news that Boney had begun
His barge-building shook everyone,   Invasion army at Boulogne
And half a million Volunteers   1804
Turned out to drill with home-made spears.

But spears could not stave off defeat:
Survival rested with the Fleet.
If it could sink the French and Spanish.
The threat would practically vanish;
If it was sunk, then so were we.
Lord Nelson's death in *Victory*,   Battle of Trafalgar 21 Oct
Which seemed to Hardy most unfair,   1805
Gave Londoners Trafalgar Square;
And Boney (let's give him his due),
Made Wellesley sweat at Waterloo.   18 Jun 1815
A Eurostar, his monument   Arthur Wellesley, Duke of
Connects us with the Continent.   Wellington 1769–1852

The Church was now a top career
Like banking, law or brewing beer:

Founded by
John Wesley
1703–91

So Methodism soon began
To cater for the common man.
The poor trudged miles to be told
By Wesley just what heaven would hold,
If only they'd pull up their socks
And put some money in the box.
This prompted thrift and application;
Which didn't always help salvation,
Since if they were a great success

Wesley's complaint 1787

They thought of heaven rather less.

King George the Third's reign left no doubt
That social change had come about;
And academic speculation
Addressed the problems of the nation.

Adam Smith, *Wealth of Nations*

To Smith, Free Trade was the solution;

Richard Price, *On Civil Liberty*

To Price, a moral revolution
Was overdue; while Bentham spread

Jeremy Bentham, *Theory of Legislation*

More Happiness on people's bread.
But most reformers worth the name
Thought Poor Laws had to take the blame –
Softness (at popular expense)
Simply encouraged Indolence.

This attitude was pretty beastly,
Though held by men like Joseph Priestley,   1733–1804
Who proved that oxygen could burn –
A lesson onlookers would learn
When all his goods went up in smoke.   Producing CO_2
The Gordon Riots were no joke: In London 2–9 Jun 1780
Distilleries were broken in,
And pavements flowed with (Gordon's?) Gin.
This flowering of anarchy   At least
Made politicians panicky: 25 were
One slip, and they'll be at our throat.   executed
And as for giving them the vote...!

It's no surprise the heavies backed
A most intimidating Act   Combination Acts 1799–1800
That banned all strikes and disputation;
And you can guess their irritation
When Wilberforce discovered ways   William Wilberforce
Of trimming children's 12-hour days   1759–1833
(Which left more time for Christian rules
To be instilled in Sunday Schools).
His reputation, though, was made
As scourge of the inhuman trade.   Owning slaves made illegal
                                          1807
He founded Freetown, where they'd bring   Capital of Sierra Leone
Bewildered slaves for counselling.

Nov 1787　King George had once talked to a tree,
Which put Pitt in a quandary;
But he regained his wits again,
Regency 1811–20　And stayed quite sane till 1810.
Later GEORGE IV 1820–30　His son, Prince Regent, lived on debt:
Around him swarmed a raffish set
Pursuing pleasure ever faster:
It was an absolute disaster.
Maria Fitzherbert 1756–1837　His first espoused was most unregal
(And, being Catholic, illegal);
Caroline of Brunswick　His next was hardly ever seen,
1768–1821　And dropped before she could be Queen.

Those Georgian houses seem so 'right'!
They had strict rules of width and height,
And to Prince George's decadence
We owe the pillared elegance
Projects of John Nash　Of Regent's Park and Royal Crescent.
1752–1835

The Palace, though, looks much less pleasant –
It too was started by John Nash,
But finally ran out of cash.
Work on the Marble Arch (intended
To be the entrance) was suspended;
And when they carried on again
They dumped the Arch up near Park Lane.   Repositioned 1851

Smart ladies went *décolletée*,
And threw their petticoats away,
And waltzed (the trendy thing to do) –
What was the country coming to?
Well, once King George the Fourth was dead   WILLIAM IV 1830–7
We floundered in a watershed:
A kind of second Reformation.
Lord Liverpool's administration,   Prime Minister 1812–27
Apart from the odd march and riot,   e.g. 'Peterloo' Massacre
Had seen the workers pretty quiet: 16 Aug 1819
But Earl Grey's stint turned out to be
A very different cup of tea.   Prime Minister 1830–34

Herbal constituent of Earl Grey tea	This devotee of bergamot
	Had trouble brewing in his pot.
	The workers, ready for a tussle,
National Union of Working Classes 1831	Began to get some useful muscle;
	The disenfranchised middle class
	Thought Parliament was just a farce –
	Old Sarum (which is always quoted)
	Had two MPs, and seven voted.
	Earl Grey's quite radical solution
	Earned votes, and smothered
	revolution:
	Though fierce the fight, he won at last –
Reform Act 1832	The Great Reform Act had been passed.

One of its aims was to transfer
MPs to towns like Manchester
And give the tiny seats the chop.
Although reforming zeal would stop
At letting women have a say,
It franchised males who had to pay

e.g. £50 per annum for tenants · So much a year in rates or rent.
This still gave only 3 per cent
The vote; but wealthy men could
stand

e.g. £300 urban property owners · Although they didn't have much land:

Grey saw how useful it would be
To have MPs from Industry.

King William's mistress had been loyal
But couldn't be considered royal;

He had 10 children by
Dorothy Jordan

He scanned the short-list someone made,
And liked the sound of Adelaide.

Adelaide of Saxe-Meiningen
1792–1849

Two girls were all that she could bear;
They soon died, leaving him no heir.
Since brother Edward (to whose head

Edward, George III's fourth
son

The crown came next) by now was dead,
His daughter, once a rank outsider,

Alexandrina Victoria
b. 24 May 1819

Sensed destiny in step beside her:
Victoria, just turned eighteen,
Would be our longest-reigning queen.

VICTORIA 1837–1901

173

'Though pearly peaks in morning's light
May the beholding eye delight,
Their brilliant summits really owe
Their shine to killing nights of snow.'
This is the way I would compare
The good and bad of *laissez-faire*.
Victorians liked to be free
From petty rules and scrutiny.

If everyone throughout the nation
Worked to improve their situation,
What they did would enhance the rest,
And all would turn out for the best!   The Utilitarian philosophy

It was an optimistic view
That manifestly wouldn't do.
Frightful injustice was appearing:
You needed social engineering   Urged by John Stuart Mill
                                       1806–73
When millions slaved their lives away
For up to fourteen hours a day.   Six days a week
Good men and women tried to speak
Against an eighty-hour week,
And hint that working folk of ten
Might gain from schooling now and then.   e.g. Lord Shaftesbury 1801–85
But *laissez-faire* did not agree:
This was the way things had to be.

But still, the poor were out of sight,
And Britain's wealth was at its height.
Two reasons: one historical,
The other geological.
Our sea-girt land had always needed
A navy, which now far exceeded
The feeble fleets of foreign forces.
And then – such natural resources!
Across our tilted mainland's spread,
The Earth's crust, heaving in its bed,
Raised strata laid down long ago:
From these, the Iron Age would flow.

Here, too, was coal to melt the ore,
Formed half a billion years before
From trees and swampy vegetation,
Now blazing in its immolation,
Extruding white-hot rails, to puff
More of this necessary stuff
To cotton mill, or factory,
Or steamships waiting at the quay
(Themselves made from the precious iron
This Revolution would rely on).
Without these, buried in our heart,
Would there have been an Age to start?

5000 miles of railway laid
1830–48

177

Let's pick the story up again
Nine years into Victoria's reign.

Tory Prime Minister 1841–46 · The great Sir Robert Peel offended
The wealthy farmers, when he ended

Corn Laws repealed 1846 · The ban on cheap imports of corn.
With this, the Liberals were born
From Whigs and 'Peelites', who
could see
That in this new democracy
The middle class had all the say.
The Tory vote just fell away:
From '46 to '74
They had five years on top –
no more.

It was 1851 feet long · Whose length equalled the date in feet?
And took just ten months to complete

Joseph Paxton, engineer 1801–65 · From Joseph Paxton's first suggestion?
It's really quite a simple question.
The local Greens had won a fight
To save three elm trees on the site

In London's Hyde Park · They'd chosen for the Exhibition.
With no alternative position
(And no sign of Dutch Elm Disease)
The plan was scuppered by those trees,

178

Till Paxton ended the impasse:
'Enclose them in a house of glass!'

Crystal Palace 1 May-15 Oct 1851

It was an absolute sensation:
A symbol of world domination.
True, Ireland's potato blight
Had killed off every plant in sight,

Approx 50% died or emigrated in 1840s

And workers seemed to want the vote
(Three million of them signed a Note).

Chartist march and petition 1842

But look at all the discontent
Enveloping the Continent!

In Austria, France, Italy, Prussia, etc. 1848

Mob rule, uprisings, stupid fuss –
Come to Hyde Park, and learn from us!
Six million did, scrubbed and clean-spoken:
And not a single window broken.

Alliance against Russia
1854–56

But soon, the war in the Crimea
Began to make the cracks appear.

William Russell 1820–1907

The *Times* reporter on the spot
Encoded into dash and dot
Descriptions of the dreadful sight,
And, almost at the speed of light,
He telegraphed a major scoop,

Government fell 1855

Which put the Army in the soup.
Its callousness caused consternation:
Disease, exposure, and starvation
Put paid to roughly half our force

Florence Nightingale
1820–1910

(Hence Florence and her Lamp, of course).

Through all this, though she was the Queen,
Victoria was rarely seen.
She'd been marked out as bride-to-be

Albert of Saxe-Coburg &
Gotha 1819–61

Of Albert since their nascency,
And though her moods were most erratic
He was extremely diplomatic.

Nine times she was induced to think
Of England; then brought to the brink
Of incoherence, when he lay
In fevered bed, and passed away.   He died aged 42, 14 Dec 1861
She disappeared from public sight
At Osborne, on the Isle of Wight.

The Tories had patched up their split,
And once more made a fight of it.
With sleek Disraeli at their head   Benjamin Disraeli 1804–81
(And called Conservatives instead)
They gave votes to a whole new section –   Reform Bill 1867
And promptly lost the next election.
Gladstone picked up the middle ground: William Gladstone 1809–98
The Liberals remained around   Prime Minister four times
Until he overplayed his hand   1868–94
And wrecked their boat on Ireland.
Victoria liked Disraeli best:
He, shrewdly, saw she was Empressed.   Pronounced Empress of India
                                                     1876

Poor Ireland! Things had not improved.

Pushed through by Pitt the Younger

An 1801 Act removed

Its Parliament; instead, it sent

MPs to Westminster, which meant

That disenfranchised Catholics swore

e.g. Fenian revolt 1867

To free themselves from British law.

To Gladstone, Irish devolution

(Or Home Rule) was the right solution:

But no way could he get that passed.

Protestants, mainly in Ulster

The Anglo-Irish were aghast:

Could any Parliament agree

To drown them in that Irish Sea?

182

What else, before our space runs out?
There's far too much to talk about!
John Forster's Education Bill;
The suffrage to more people still;
Police to keep the crime rate down;
Gas bringing light to every town;
And every Sunday, giving praise
To God for showing them His ways!
It's fashionable now to sneer,
But were they really insincere?
Don't be too eager to condemn –
Born earlier, we'd all be them.

Elementary education for all
1870
In 1884–5; but not to women

'Victorian hypocrisy'

183

House of Saxe-Coburg & Gotha
1901—10

Prince of Wales b. 1841

Prince Edward, from his youth, was wild –
A most uncompromising child
Who banged his head against the wall,
And wouldn't do his sums at all.
They boxed his ears, swished the cane,
Refused him playmates: all in vain.
When he became too big to beat,
They read him poems as a treat,
And let him gaze on works of art
To soften that rebellious heart.

Ungrateful children are a curse —
The people liked him, which was worse.

Bertie, as he was called, would be
The public face of royalty
In Mother's forty years of mourning,
Although she gave him ample warning
That she did not find him amusing,
What with his racing, cards and boozing
(Plus other things best left unsaid).
As Britain's Prince, then King, he led
The waltzing, jewelled, champagne set
That surfed in Europe's Internet,
Where everyone knew who was who.
Ten kings were linked by marriage, too.

Christened Albert Edward

Especially Alice Keppel
1869–1947
EDWARD VII 1901–10

Those glittering Edwardian days
Are now seen as the final phase
Of Britain's rule by an élite.
The House of Lords, which could
    defeat
All Commons Bills up to that date
Could now only prevaricate;
And promptings of a new direction
Emerged at the '06 election,
When thirty new MPs began

Birth of the Labour Party

To represent the working man.
(If they had not been taught to read,
They wouldn't know they had a need.)

Trade now struck problems everywhere:
It was no time for *laissez-faire*.
The USA had learned to dump
Its corn on us, which caused a slump
By undercutting farmers' prices;
Our exports, also, were in crisis,
Since foreigners, behind our backs,
Were slapping on an import tax.

MacKinley import tariff 1890

America put up the shutters;
The Germans next (which caused some
    mutters);

But still we struggled to resist
The call to go Protectionist.

The king was dead: behind the carriage   Edward's funeral 20 May 1910
Marched Wilhelm, nephew by the marriage   Kaiser Wilhelm r. 1888–1918
Of Edward's sister Vicky, who
Had caused a real hullabaloo
By falling for a Prussian prince
And speaking German ever since.
With Wilhelm strode his royal cousin
King George V; almost a dozen   GEORGE V 1910–36
Crowned heads (each one of them descended
From Queen Victoria) attended.
The closest families fall out:
And this one would, without a doubt.

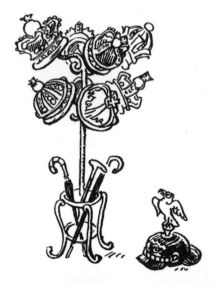

House of Windsor 1910—Present

What started off the First World War?
It had to happen, as a thaw
That rises only one degree
May start an avalanche. Let's see…

Under Bismarck 1871

The German states had coalesced,
(Though Prussia overawed the rest),

Triple alliance (with Italy)
1882

And gave the Austrians their backing
In case the Russians came attacking.

Pact of 1894

Russia and France swore mutual aid;
And Austria was now afraid
Of conquered Serbia to the east.
Unstable times, to say the least.

Our stance was 'splendid isolation';
But gradually the situation
Began to change, when Germany
Showed signs of planning war at sea
By laying down a whole new fleet.
Here was a threat we had to meet.
The Kaiser simply brushed away

i.e. cease all new shipbuilding

Our proffered 'naval holiday'
(In other words, we'd keep the edge),
And with our very public pledge

To France and Russia, it was clear
There was no going back from here.

This stanza's taken me some time –
Such very awkward words to rhyme.
Gavrilo Princip was the one
Who fired the World War's starting gun.
In Sarajevo, by the kerb,
This revolutionary Serb
Stood waiting, pistol in his hand,
For Austria's Archduke Ferdinand.
The driver, though, had lost his way;
Gavrilo went to a café,
Then saw the Archduke's car outside –
He couldn't have missed him if he'd tried.

Triple Entente 1905–7

A postman's son 1895–1918

28 Jun 1914

The Germans' Schlieffen Plan advised
That Belgium should be neutralized.
According to a pact we swore
Just seventy-five years before,
We'd rise at once to the occasion
If Belgium suffered an invasion.

War declared 11 pm on
4 Aug 1914

There wasn't much that we could do;
However, as in World War Two,
We tried our best. Our grimmest thoughts
Concerned the vital Channel ports:
For once the Germans ruled the sea
There was no telling where we'd be.

This land war was completely new.
Our last great battle, Waterloo,

Had been of the old-fashioned sort
Where compact armies met and fought
In some indignant farmer's field,
Until one side was forced to yield.
Now, using railways, they spread
Their armies in long lines instead,
Which meant no 'battle' could begin.
The two sides simply got dug in:
Barbed wire stretched its bloody strand
From Antwerp down to Switzerland.

They stood in lines to claim their right
To take part in this virtuous fight:
Three quarters of a million needed

20,000 killed on 1 Jul 1916 alone

To be mown down, their flower unseeded.
But nought is nothing. Simply stand
In any village in the land,
And read the random names of those
Whose richer dust more surplus grows.

Rupert Brooke: *The Soldier*

Did such loss justify the cause
(To win the war to end all wars),
Its only everlasting gain
Those acres sacred to the slain?

War ended 11 Nov 1918

One social outcome of the war
Was bringing women to the fore:
With men in millions in the trenches
They started working at the benches

And throughout industry

To make the cartridges required
Whenever shots had to be fired.

The Suffragette movement

The suffragettes smashed window panes,
Banged heads, and threw themselves at trains;
But Votes for Women came to pass
Through labour, not by broken glass.

At thirty they could join the line –
Or go on being twenty-nine.

Representation of the People
Act 1918

The twenties – were they really Gay
(Before its old sense passed away)?
Dresses with waists below their knees,
But very little shape to please;
Suave men in flannels, stripes, and boater;
And being called for in the motor…
Yes – but beneath those careless feet,
The miners sweated in the heat
For lower pay, as profits fell;
And unemployment rose as well.
The General Strike had no effect –

4–12 May 1926

The world recession went unchecked.

The Irish saga blundered on.

In 1914 Home Rule had been agreed upon,

Though no one, in their heart of hearts,

Saw hope of merging its two parts.

It wasn't, therefore, too surprising

Inspired by Roger Casement When rebels staged the Easter Rising
1916

Against the Anglo-Irish side.

Sinn Féin ('ourselves alone') then tried

Irish Free State Dec 1921 To give birth to an Irish nation

Led by Eamon de Valera Divorced from British legislation.
1882–1975

Partition was the only way:

Republic of Eire created 1949 The problem's with us still today.

Our politics were in transition:
Most governments were coalition,
Since urgent times urge urgent courses,
And rivals readily join forces.
The Liberals, with Asquith, ran

Herbert Asquith
PM 1908–16

The country till the war began;
A coup by Lloyd George sent him packing

David Lloyd George
PM 1916–22

(Since he'd lost everybody's backing);
Conservatives then had a bash
Until the famous Wall Street Crash.

Oct 1929: led to the
Depression

Joint government resumed once more,
And lasted through the second war.

King George the Fifth did what was right:
And though his reign does not excite,
He'd check the atmospheric pressure,
And note down if the wind was fresher.
His naval beard and sailor's bearing,
The peaked cap he was fond of wearing,
Suggest a captain on the bridge
Concerned about the pilotage.
But think how few had ever seen,
Let alone *heard*, a king or queen;
So what could have been more dramatic
Than his faint voice in all that static?

First Christmas broadcast 1932

Though Father had been most correct,

EDWARD VIII
20 Jan–11 Dec 1936

Edward, the Prince of Wales, wrecked

The royal image. His delight

b. Wallis Warfield 1896–1986

In Mrs Simpson, socialite,

American, and married twice,

Was not considered very nice.

So Edward, to secure his mate,

Made up his mind to abdicate,

And, as the Duke of Windsor, went

With Wallis into banishment –

A strong hint that it doesn't do

GEORGE VI 1936–52

To fall for blood that isn't blue.

But now a chilly wind was blowing

From Europe: German strength was growing.

The Versailles Treaty stripped them bare: Post-war settlement 1919
No colonies left anywhere;
The most colossal bill to pay
(They borrowed from the USA);
And not a single ship or plane.
A most unsavoury campaign
Made Hitler Chancellor, then Führer.   Adolf Hitler 1889–1945
He trod on treaties, and grew sührer
That since we wanted him Appeased
He might as well do as he pleased.

Austria (Anschluss)
12 Mar 1938
Czechoslovakia Sep 1938

Neville Chamberlain PM
1937–40

War declared 3 Sep 1939

Dunkirk evacuation
May–Jun 1940

p.157

Winston Churchill 1874–1965

The Austrians, and then the Czechs,
Were nations Adolf would annexe:
At Munich, for a year's delay,
We signed the Czechs' own lands away.
The Poles were next, and we'd agreed
To fight for them in case of need
(Though since they'd quickly signed a truce,
Our help was not the slightest use).
Our Expeditionary Force
In France seemed doomed; and then, of course,
Dunkirk's impromptu rescue fleet
Gilded unqualified defeat.

When mentioning the Elder Pitt
I wrote (I'm rather proud of it):
Impossible to have about,
Impossible to do without.
That was the fairly widespread view
Of Winston Churchill's colleagues, too.

His strategy made experts groan;
He couldn't leave things well alone –
No matter! In the public sphere
He spoke the words we longed to hear.
He strove for peace, but thrilled to war:
He was, he said, the Lion's Roar.

Became PM (Con)
10 May 1940

The Germans, having tried persuasion,
Now started planning an invasion,
But needed, as a guarantee,
Clear air superiority.
So Göring left off bombing homes
And started hitting aerodromes
(For there is really no denying
That planes are far more useful flying).
A medieval tournament
Stretched ribbons through the skies of Kent:
The knightly Few who fought for us,
Each strapped inside his Pegasus.

Head of the Luftwaffe
(Air Force)

'Battle of Britain'
Aug–Sep 1940

Impatient with mere runway hits,
Göring decided on a Blitz,
And set the capital ablaze

Blitz 7 Sep 1940–10 May 1941 On fifty-seven sequent days.
Besieged and battered, Churchill fought
To get American support

US President 1932–45 From Roosevelt, and through Lend-Lease
They sent us aid, though still at peace.
But sinkings crossing the Atlantic

By German U-boats
(submarines) Were driving everybody frantic:
Supplies of fuel, corn for bread –
Could Hitler starve us out instead?

Pearl Harbor, that uncouth event,
Was, from our viewpoint, heaven-sent.
Japan and Germany had signed
A pact by which they were aligned,
Which meant that Adolf, right away,
Declared war on the USA;
Though what with fighting Russians too,
It seemed a crazy thing to do.
(The 'Axis' nations numbered three,
The other being Italy:
Captain Corelli's Mandolin
Describes the state that they were in.)

Churchill was worried that the Yanks,
Who'd started mass-producing tanks,
Might seek revenge for their mishaps
By concentrating on the Japs.
But helping Britain on the brink
Had served to forge a common link.
Stalin, whose style was pretty blunt,
Insisted on a Second Front,
But at that time there was no chance
Of doing anything in France;
And so we battled in the Med,
And crawled up Italy instead.

Japanese attack on USA
7 Dec 1941

Attacked Russia 22 Jun 1941

Joseph Stalin, USSR,
1879–1953

Sicily invaded Jul 1943

Normandy
landings
6 Jun 1944

D-Day arrived (I've skipped a lot),
So Adolf had one final shot
By launching, in their deadly curve,
The V2s, planned to break our nerve.
But like our own raids, day and night,

e.g. Hamburg
27–28 Jul 1943

Which turned the very air alight,
Reducing people's homes to rubble
Just caused unnecessary trouble,
And left a legacy of hate.
This was the lamentable fate
Of fragile Dresden, which became

Incinerated 13–14 Feb 1945

A medieval ball of flame.

Victory in Europe
8 May 1945

VE Day: down the Mall, to see
The royals on the balcony!
George, the most diffident of kings,
Was thrown into the thick of things

When brother Edward abdicated.
But public outrage soon abated –
Here was a man we could rely on.
Lady Elizabeth Bowes-Lyon
(His long-lived wife, our monarch's mother)
Stood by him in the smoke and smother
Of gaping London: they were hit
Eight times, and seemed to relish it.

1900–2002 (married 1923)

The war was won; but would the cost
Have been much greater if we'd lost?
Wrecked cities, rationing, no fuel
(And winters in those years were cruel);
Too deep in debt to pay our way,
Hence more loans from the USA...
Gas, coal, the trains, electric light
Were nationalized overnight
With Labour in. They also thought
They'd back the Beveridge Report,
Which blueprinted the Welfare State:
Free health-care, and no need to wait.

Clement Attlee PM 1945–51

National Health Service
Act 1946

Atom bombs on Hiroshima
and Nagasaki Aug 1945

ELIZABETH II crowned
2 Jun 1953

£700m from the USA in 1947

Prescription charges 1951

Two air-bursts had eclipsed the sun
Over Japan; now everyone
Who saw the photographs, could see
Uranium's capacity
For cost-effective devastation,
Plus bonus deaths from radiation.
As Cold War temperatures congealed,
Blue Streak became our spear and shield,
Deterring others from beginning
A war we had no hope of winning –
The daft thing took so long to prime,
It couldn't have been launched in time.

Our young Queen's festive coronation
Was tinsel on a bankrupt nation.
We'd had a dole of Marshall Aid
(Which didn't have to be repaid);
But interest on the millions owing,
Plus keeping all that Welfare going,
Plus the fantastic costs inherent
In building up our own deterrent,
Led to a gut-wrenching repeal
Of Labour's Socialist ideal:
To ease our economic ills,
People would have to pay for pills.

Strong exports were the only way
The country could be made to pay,
But Germany, with massive aid,
Had jumped ahead of us in trade:
The Japs were getting in there too –
You'll notice that they never queue!
We should have joined the EEC
When it was in its infancy,

Original Six 1957

And when at last we had a go
We got that legendary *No*
(In French) from Charles de Gaulle himself:
'Stay on the Continental Shelf!'

Application
rejected 1963

Revolt over prescriptions meant
The end of Labour's government.
Their innovations, though, would last
Till after our time-span is past –
The NHS is with us still,
To cheer us when we're feeling ill.
Churchill, returned, did not inspire.

Winston Churchill
PM 1951–5

His world was gone: the Empire
Had now begun to fall apart,
Which broke his patriarchal heart.

e.g. India's independence
1947

He'd lived his life, and fought his war:
His last words? 'Everything's a bore.'

Died 24 Jan 1965

This era saw a housing boom
(Though tower blocks took up less room),
And now a major spending spree

Seeds of later 'boom and bust'

Inflated the economy.
But Britain was humiliated

Anthony Eden (Con) 1955–7

At Suez: Eden instigated
A raid to annexe the Canal
And make it international.
He quit because of all the flak.

Harold Macmillan (Con) 1957–63

Then came the years of Supermac:
Posh accent, stooping, old school tie –
The perfect butt for *Private Eye*.

He got on well with Kennedy,
Whose nuclear diplomacy
Made hearts around the planet quake.
But Khrushchev's nerve was first to break –
The Cuban missiles departed.
The Swinging Sixties had now started…
You thought four-letter words obscene?
No! *Lady Chatterley* was clean,
Which meant it was all right to say
Just what you liked, in book or play;
While mini-skirts hid less and less,
Till there was nothing left to guess.

Bob Dylan's lyrics caught the mood;
The Beatles made a hit with *Jude*;
The goalposts widened overnight:
'Don't worry – it'll be all right!'
But how could either of you know
How far you really ought to go?
Hot baths and gin: and then get married
If after that she's not miscarried…
The chastened groom, his bulging bride;
Their parents smiling, mortified:
'This should have been a happy day!
What will our friends and neighbours say?'

John Kennedy, US President
1961–3

Cuban missile crisis
Oct–Nov 1962
Soviet Premier 1958–64

Obscenity trial 1960

First LP *Please Please Me*
Feb 1963

Those gunshots from the Dallas store
Would fix in mind for evermore
When we received the intimation

By Lee Harvey Oswald
22 Nov 1963

Of Kennedy's assassination.
The BBC announcer cried:
It felt as if a friend had died.
But now I've reached 'remembered' time,
I'll end my convoluted rhyme
With Bobby Moore lifting up

England 4 Germany 2,
Wembley 30 July 1966

The 1966 World Cup
When England took their Final bow:
'They think it's over – it is now!'

Postscript

I thought I'd end our story on a high.
And anyway, from now on my perspective
Is personal: however hard I try,
It's very difficult to be objective.
The pound devalued to relieve inflation;
The Three-Day Week; the years of boom
      and bust;
The Falklands War; the Irish conflagration;
Diana's death left everyone concussed…
The tides of destiny that drive us on
(Too deep to fathom, or too close to see)
Cannot be analysed until they've gone –
When we shall all be Rhyming History.

The Kings and Queens of England

Houses of Cerdic and Denmark

927–939	Athelstan
939–946	Edmund I
946–955	Eadred
955–959	Eadwig
959–975	Edgar I
975–978	Edward I (The Martyr)
978–1016	Ethelred (The Unready)
1016	Edmund II
1016–35	Canute
1035–40	Harold I
1040–42	Harthacnut
1042–66	Edward II (The Confessor)
1066	Harold II

House of Normandy

1066–87	William I (The Conqueror)
1087–1100	William II (Rufus)
1100–35	Henry I
1135–54	Stephen

House of Anjou (Plantagenets)

1154–89	Henry II
1189–99	Richard I (The Lionheart)
1199–1216	John
1216–72	Henry III
1272–1307	Edward I (Longshanks)
1307–27	Edward II (Isabella & Mortimer 1327–30)
1327–77	Edward III
1377–99	Richard II

House of Lancaster

1399–1413	Henry IV
1413–22	Henry V
1422–61, 1470–71	Henry VI

House of York

1461–70, 1471–83	Edward IV
1483	Edward V
1483–85	Richard III

House of Tudor

1485–1509	Henry VII
1509–47	Henry VIII
1547–53	Edward VI
1553	Jane
1553–58	Mary I (Bloody Mary)
1558–1603	Elizabeth I

House of Stuart

1603–25	James I
1625–49	Charles I (Commonwealth 1649–60)
1660–85	Charles II
1685–88	James II
1689–1702	William III & Mary II (d. 1694)
1702–14	Anne

The author s English mnemonic

Conquering William (No. 1)
Left the country to his son
William No. 2 (the Red),
Shot by accident, it's said.
Henry, Stephen, Henry 2;
Richard (Lionheart to you);
Craven John, then Henry 3;
After him, a dynasty
Of Edwards (1–3), although
Isabella stole the show
With Mortimer, for three mad years.
Mighty Edward 3 appears;
Richard 2 and Henry 4;
Henry 5 of Agincourt;
Feeble Henry 6 defeated

By Edward 4, who sort of cheated;
Edward 5 died in the Tower
(Crookback Richard's bid for power);
Henry 7, Henry 8
(Got through wives at quite a rate),
Edward 6 was young and sickly;
Nine-day Jane beheaded quickly
By Bloody Mary, who dismissed her,
And was succeeded by her sister
Elizabeth! James followed next,
Then Charles, who was extremely vexed
When Oliver removed his head
And tried to run the place instead.
Charles the Second reinstated;
James the Second widely hated;
William 3 was the solution,
Thanks to bloodless revolution;
He left his widow Mary crowned.
Anne, her sister, stayed around
Till the Georges (1–4)
And one more William, held the door
For Queen Victoria, who'd thought
Her chances of the throne were nought!
Seventh Edward boozed and bedded;
George the Fifth was level-headed;
Love-sick Edward No 8
Felt he had to abdicate;
So George the Sixth would fit the bill
Until our Queen, who's reigning still!

The Kings and Queens of Scotland

1005–34	Malcolm II
1034–40	Duncan I
1040–57	Macbeth
1057–58	Lulach
1058–93	Malcolm III
1093–94,	
1094–97	Donald III
1094	Duncan II
1097–1107	Edgar
1107–24	Alexander I
1124–53	David I
1153–65	Malcolm IV
1165–1214	William I
1214–49	Alexander II
1249–86	Alexander III
1286–90	Margaret

(1290–2 Interregnum)

House of Balliol

1292–96	John

(1296–1306 Interregnum)

House of Bruce

1306–29	Robert I
1329–32,	
1336–71	David II
	(Edward Balliol 1332–36)

House of Stewart

1371–90	Robert II
1390–1406	Robert III
1406–37	James I
1437–60	James II
1460–88	James III
1488–1513	James IV
1513–42	James V
1542–67	Mary (Queen of Scots)
1567–1625	James VI

Monarchs shared with England 1603–1707.

The author's Scottish mnemonic

Malcolm Two began the line.
Duncan, next, was doing fine
Till Macbeth seized bloody power.
Lulach lasted half an hour;
Malcolm Three in battle slain
(Four of his own sons would reign).

Donald Three was told to stop;
Duncan Two received the chop;
Edgar, Alexander, Dave;
Malcolm Four, William the Brave;
Alexanders Two and Three;
Margaret, Queen in infancy.
John of Balliol was next,
Crowned on England's sly pretext;
Then came Robert's House of Bruce.
David Two was not much use
In the procreative bed,
So the Stewarts reigned instead.
Roberts Two and Three, then James,
After which, no other names
Till the fifth one in succession
Left poor Mary in possession.
James the Sixth and last, her son,
Would be England's No. 1!

SHAKESPEARE IN A NUTSHELL

A RHYMING GUIDE TO ALL THE PLAYS

Romeo and Juliet

The *Sonnet* is the form I will select
To tell this story of extreme devotion:
Two young lives (not to mention others) wrecked
Because they couldn't handle their emotion.
Romeo thrives on Love's ecstatic pain —
The more it hurts, the more he is elated;
Fair Rosaline has put him off again,
Leaving the lad exquisitely frustrated! [I, i]
Now Fate takes him in hand: he goes off, masked,
To revels in the home of Capulet, [I, v]
Where Montagues (his name) are never asked;
And here the lad's knocked out
    by Juliet . . .
Their gaze sinks deeper than
    the sharpest blade,
Their lips touch, and the fatal
    contract's made!

He's in her orchard; she comes into view, [II, ii]
Presumably about to go to bed:
'Why do you have to be a *Montague*?
Why couldn't you be Smith or Brown instead?' [II, ii, 33]

Well, everybody knows what happens then:
She titillates him from her balcony,
Going inside and coming back again!
So now we move directly to Scene 3,
When Romeo to Friar Lawrence
     speeds   [II, iii]
To fix their rites as soon as he
     is able,
And finds him gathering what
     look like weeds,
Whose essence (with directions
     on the label)
This holy man distils, and people use
To mimic Death and wake up when they choose![†]

I'm bothered by the enigmatic Nurse,
Who helps this ill-starred match to go ahead,
And (when we reach a slightly later verse)
Lets down the coiled rope to Juliet's bed!
She is a cheerful soul, but seems to me
Ambivalent, an agent of destruction:
It's quite incredible if she can't see
That this defiant act will cause disruption . . .
But anyway, she serves the lovers well,
And tells her charge that things have been arranged:
The two must meet at Friar Lawrence's cell
To have their vows officially exchanged.

[†] Juliet uses some, prepared from flowers
  That lay her out for two and forty hours.   [IV, i]

This may, the Friar thinks, help to unite
Their families — and in a way he's right!

His married status kept in secrecy,
Romeo waits for night and Consummation . . . [III, i]
But here is Tybalt, his worst enemy —
A Capulet of no great toleration.
'Draw, villain!' Tybalt cries, infuriated
By Romeo's gate-crashing in
    Act 1;
But Romeo smiles, because
    they're now related,
And fighting cousins simply
    isn't done.
Mercutio, Romeo's friend,
    thinks he's gone soft.
'I'll thrash this fellow if you
    won't!' he cries,
Unable to endure being scoffed
By strutting Tybalt; but he's stabbed, and dies —
So Romeo slays Tybalt in contrition,
Which puts him in a difficult position . . .

Now trouble's brewing! Romeo's banishèd
(Pronounce the 'e') in all the hullabaloo,
And to the friendly Friar's cell he's fled — [III, iii]
The poor man's never had so much to do.

'Cheer up, my son. The Prince
    has been forgiving.
Banishment's mercy!' 'Beyond Verona's
    walls,   [III, iii, 17]
If Juliet's within, life's not worth living.
Banishment's worse than death.' 'Oh —
    utter nonsense!

Tonight enjoy with her; but, in disguise,
At break of day to Mantua depart,
Where you'll be well concealed from
    vengeful eyes
Till Prince and parents have a change of heart!'
The rope ladder [†] the newlyweds unites . . .
It's fortunate he has a head for heights!

Romeo is awoken by a bird.
'*Lullula arborea* — time to go!'   [III, v, 6]
'No, dearest, it's *Luscinia* you heard —
There's quite a difference, as you ought to know!'
'Now look,' says Romeo: 'I've
    got to flee
To Mantua right now,
    while it's still dark,
Not argue about
    Ornithology:
That *wasn't* a nightingale
    — it was a lark!'

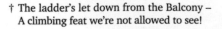

---

† The ladder's let down from the Balcony –
  A climbing feat we're not allowed to see!

So off to exile from beloved Verona;
And Juliet is simply horrified
When told she's due to have a
second owner —

Count Paris is to take her as
his bride!
Her natural reaction is 'Oh, hell!'
So back again to Friar Lawrence's cell . . .

To fix the date, the Friar's had a visit   [IV, i]
From Paris. The desperate girl begins to cry.
'It's not a very good beginning, is it?
Don't make me marry *him*! I'd rather die!'   [IV, i, 50]
Her desperation moves the harassed Friar:
'Of this distillèd liquor (say the 'e')
I'll let you have the dose you will require
To seem to lie in death's extremity.

Romeo and Juliet

Take it the night before your wedding day:
You'll be interrèd in the ancient vault
Where all your lot go when they pass away.
Then, with your marriage cancelled by default,
We'll whisk you off to join your banished lord,
And you'll find somewhere nice to live abroad!'

Although it sounds a slightly risky scheme,
They go for it, for want of something better.
This part of the intrigue works like a dream . . .   [IV, v]
But there's a problem, since the vital letter
The Friar writes to Romeo, to say
What's going on, does not reach his address;
So we can sympathize with his dismay
When her demise is bruited. What a mess!   [V, i]
Life has no meaning without Juliet . . .
To her dark monument by night he'll fly
With the most potent poison he can get,
Embrace her for the final time — and die.
And so Confusion's masterpiece we'll see
Within the sepulchre — Act 5 Scene 3!

Paris comes first. His flowery tribute's scattered;   [V, iii]
But Romeo, mistaking the intruder,
Kills him, and feels absolutely shattered
To find it is the nobleman who wooed her.

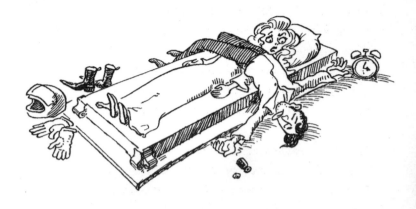

A kiss — some parting words — the poison
   swallowed . . .
He falls across the body of his mate . . .
His death, of course, immediately followed
By Juliet's yawn and stretching, just too late!
She plants the happy dagger in her breast,
And dies a second death, immortalized;
The Friar's machinations are confessed;
The postal services are criticized;
Her statue will be ordered right away —
Presumably the families will pay?

If you enjoyed reading James Muirden's witty rhymes, why not order a copy of _Shakespeare in a Nutshell_?

SHAKESPEARE IN A NUTSHELL

James Muirden, with decorations by David Eccles

A Rhyming Guide to All the Plays

It's a pretty safe bet
That you know Juliet
Has a Balcony Scene in her play ...
and which Prince cannot see
That it's better To Be ...
And which King gives his kingdom away.

But the Bard wrote far more
(Thirty something's the score);
And only an utter fanatic
Will have seen everyone –
Some plays grim, others fun,
But all, in the full sense, _dramatic_.

In this volume you've got
An account of each plot
In delicate versification,
With acts, scenes and quotes,
Plus poetical notes –
And Eccles' inspired decoration!

James Muirden, unrepentant rhymester, has now turned his pen to another British treasure – Shakespeare – and has distilled each of his thirty-eight plays into a few witty and illuminating verses.

Constable
1-84119-968-0
£9.99

Also available to order
from Constable & Robinson

WHEN IT HAPPENED

George Chamier

A Very Short History of Britain describing all the kings and queens, the principal battles and other major events, with their dates, to help anyone who can't remember or never learned.

Do you know: how the Welsh got hammered, Scotland was cleared, and England got its name? Which Roman emperor was born in Yorkshire? Why King John got the nickname 'softsword'?

From the famous battles that defined the nation to the almost forgotten events and people that contributed to the twists and turns of Britain's narrative. *When It Happened* is a clear, wry account that connects all the great dates in history and puts them in order, to show 2,000 years of our nation's story from the Roman invasion to the Falklands War.

Constable
1-84529-447-5
£9.99

CAUTIONARY VERSES AND RUTHLESS RHYMES FOR MODERN TIMES

Charlie Ottley

**'Charlie Ottley does for Belloc what the Germans did for the Mini – he has revived a classic form ... Great fun!'
Quentin Crewe**

The tragic tale of Sally Platt, who liked to chat and chat and chat (on her mobile phone of course), and the dreadful fate of Little James, who just adored computer games, feature in this collection of Charlie Ottley's new cautionary rhymes for our times. Ottley locates our Achilles' heel and goes for it with a tickling stick. From the dangers of skipping off school to over-dependence on TV soaps, these witty warnings are hugely enjoyable.

Available from November 2006

Constable
1-85429-280-4
£9.99

Order form over page

No. of copies	Title	Price	Total
	POSTAGE AND PACKING	£1.00	£1.00
	Shakespeare in a Nutshell James Muirden	£9.99	
	Cautionary Verses and Ruthless Rhymes Charlie Ottley (available from November 2006)	£9.99	
	When it Happened George Chamier	£9.99	
	Grand Total		**£**

Name . . . .

Address . . . .

. . . .

Postcode . . . .

Daytime Tel. No./Email . . . .
(in case of query)

Three ways to pay:

1 **For express service telephone the TBS order line on 01206 255 800 and quote 'RH1'. Order lines are open Monday–Friday 8:30 a.m. – 5:30p.m.**

2 I enclose a cheque made payable to **TBS** Ltd for £____

3 Please charge my ❑ Visa ❑ Mastercard ❑ Amex

❑ Switch (switch issue no . . . .) £____

Card number . . . .

Expiry date . . . . Signature . . . .
(your signature is essential when paying by credit card)

Please return forms (*no stamps required*) to,
FREEPOST RLUL-SJGC-SGKJ, Cash Sales/Direct Mail Dept,
The Book Service, Colchester Road, Frating, Colchester, CO7 7DW

Enquiries to readers@constablerobinson.com
www.constablerobinson.com

Constable & Robinson (directly or via its agents) may mail or phone you about promotions or products.

Tick box if you do not want these from us ❑ or our subsidiaries ❑.